HAUNTED FLORIDA PANHANDLE

KATLYN JONES

Haunted America

Published by Haunted America
A Division of The History Press
Charleston, SC
www.historypress.com

First published 2024

Manufactured in the United States

ISBN 9781467155762

Library of Congress Control Number: 2024936746

DEDICATIONS

FOR MY LATE GRANDPARENTS Mark and Shirley Jones. You both were such remarkable individuals, and I will forever be grateful for your love. Each of your acts of love and dedication to your family, friends and church were truly inspirational. I genuinely believe that my grandparents helped mold me into the woman I am today. They each showed me what patience, love, protection and strength are all about. Even though they are both gone from this world, I cannot thank them enough for constantly showing up for me when I needed support, helping me when I would fall, loving me when I wasn't the most lovable person and for being the most genuine people I've ever been around. Thank you, especially, to my grandma Shirley for being my best friend and a mother figure to me when I needed it most. Nothing could have broken our bond. Your words of encouragement and support have always held a special place in my heart. Thank you for truly believing in me as well as my talent for writing. I am honored to say, "I did it, Grandma!" I have officially written my first book, and I am so incredibly proud of this milestone that I have conquered. When I lost each of my grandparents, my whole world changed, and for a split second,

Mark and Shirley Jones, author's grandparents. *Author photo.*

I lost hope. I want this book to be an example of my growth and strength. I have accomplished something many never get the chance to do. Grandma and Papaw, I will forever cherish our memories within me, as you both truly left footprints on my heart. It is my mission that I, too, will leave footprints on as many people's hearts as you two did. I love you.

FOR MY BEST FRIEND and favorite author, Nicole Beauchamp. Nic, the amount of love, positivity and pure joy that radiates off you is truly incredible. The strength that you continue to have when all odds are against you inspires me daily. I am honored to have someone like you in my life, truly. You not only helped inspire me to write this book, but you also encouraged me to chase my dreams, even through all the negativity that comes with chasing one's dreams. Thank you for always having my best interests at heart and wanting the best for me. I seriously could not have done this without you and your constant support in my life. I love you.

Author Katlyn Jones's best friend, author Nicole Beauchamp. *Courtesy of Amy Shabluk (Portraits by Amy Michelle).*

FOR MY FORMER COLLEGE professor Patti Woodham. Thank you for believing in my talent and encouraging me to pursue writing. Your words of encouragement have always been with me, and I will continue to carry them with me. Thank you for making a difference in my life. I will never forget it.

CONTENTS

16. Escambia County

ACKNOWLEDGEMENTS

Firstly, I would like to thank the team at The History Press. I will never forget this milestone in my life. I am so incredibly thankful for this team, along with all the work each of you put into making this a reality for me. Thank you for helping me achieve the title of author.

To my mothers: my late birth mother, Roberta; my mother, Janna; my stepmother, Victoria; and my late grandmother Shirley. To my fathers: my father, Mark; my stepfather, Don; and my late grandfather Mark. To my siblings: Savannah, Cris, Stephanie, Kevin, Tanya, Chris, my late brother Adam and so many more. To all my lovely aunts, uncles, nieces, nephews and cousins. Thank you each for your love. You all have had such a special impact on my life, and I could not be more thankful for what our family means to me.

To Nicole Beauchamp, my closest friend, thank you sincerely. Thank you for always believing in me, loving me and wanting the best for me. I love you so much, and I could not be prouder to have you in my life.

To Benjamin Wilburn, thank you for being authentically yourself and for all the support you have given me during the process of writing this book. I deeply appreciate you being a part of my life and for making each day worth it. I love you. I'd also like to thank you for your interview with me regarding Gulf Correctional Institution.

To Carl Pence, firstly, thank you for telling me all about your experiences in an interview. I deeply appreciate all the positive things that you brought into my life, as I will never forget all the good memories that we have shared together and your always being here for me when I need a friend. Thanks for believing in this book and believing in me. I appreciate you and love you, Carl.

Benjamin and Carl, thanks for being a part of our paranormal team, Mysteries of the Unseen. The adventures we have are what make life so much more enjoyable. I appreciate all that you both do for the team.

To a sweet girl named Emma Pence, you hold such a special place in my heart. I thank you for believing in me and my book. Your passion for history and even the paranormal is astonishing. I am so proud of the person you are becoming. I hope I made you proud by writing this book. I love you, Em.

To my dear friends Celine and Johnnie Ballew. Thank you for the support and love you two have always given me. I cherish each of you, and I hope you both know how much I love you.

To all my *Call of Duty* friends, including Brittney, Lexie, Jazz, Chris and his kids, John, Curly, Blue, Zilla, Mizure, Havok, Victor, Hotshot, Henry, Fred, Nathaniel, Jon and Heather and her children, Chloe and J.D. I appreciate each of you for being with me as I embark on this journey.

To my friend Bobby Jereb. Thank you for all the support you have shown me throughout writing this book. I appreciate all your efforts in making a lovely logo for me. I cherish your work and our friendship.

To my friend Amy Shabluk. Thank you for your beautiful headshot photograph of the gorgeous author Nicole Beauchamp. If anyone is in the Michigan area, I would love for you to check out Amy's work, as she is so talented. Amy, thank you for all your help. I deeply appreciate your support with my book and your believing in my work as an author.

A huge shoutout and thanks to my photographer and dear friend Jacob Whitfield. Your work is incredible, and I feel extremely grateful for your help with photos of locations throughout this book. The lengths to which you went to get the perfect shots for me is very much appreciated. Keep pursuing your dreams and keep up the great work, friend. You got this! Anyone needing a rad photographer within the Bay County area or within the northwestern region of Florida, please check Jacob out.

Another huge thanks to Forgotten Coast Photography by Layla Marie for my lovely headshot and the photo of me walking into my next journey on the enchanting property of Wakulla Springs. I would like to encourage anyone interested in photos within the Wakulla area to reach out to Layla and let her know that author Katlyn Jones sent you her way!

Big thanks to the Bay County Library for information regarding the county's history and for providing photos, as well, for the Bay County chapter.

Big thanks to Emerald Coast Paranormal Concepts. Your team has been extremely helpful throughout this book. Thank you each for your time and efforts in helping me learn more about Jackson County, Marianna and the entire Panhandle.

McKenzie Hill, thank you for your interview and for sharing your experiences at the Russ House.

Christopher Johnson, thank you for your time and effort with your interview and for giving me more insight on Hard Labor Creek.

Whitney and Oliver Marks, thank you for your interviews and information regarding Hard Labor Creek.

Many thanks to the creators of various YouTube videos, as they helped me a lot during my research. These videos are cited in the bibliography.

Thank you, Mike Smith, for sharing your experience of Castle Dracula with me.

Thanks to Paul Bonnette, also, for sharing your experience for the Bay County chapter.

Alley Walker, thanks for your public comment found on the Backpackerverse.com website related to the Martin House.

Jonathan Ramer, thanks for reaching out about the Martin House.

Tasha Maines, thanks for your amazing story about the Martin House.

Devin Bush, thank you for your interview and your time explaining the experience you had with the Martin House.

Samantha Vereecke, thank you for your interview and information about the Pensacola Lighthouse.

Penny Lane, thank you for your interview, the information you shared and your willingness to assist me in any way with the Edward Ball Wakulla Springs Lodge. I deeply appreciate all that you have done for me.

Paul Sackman, thank you for your time and your story about O'Zone Pizza Pub.

Jennifer Stanley, thank you for your interview about the Port Saint Joe Courthouse.

Tanner Brown, thank you for your interview and sharing your story with me on Gulf Correctional Insitution.

Big thanks to Gary Yordon for granting me permission to use your gorgeous photo of the John Denham House in my book. I have a deep appreciation for great photographic work like yours.

Michael Blain, thank you for your informative and educational ghost tour and entertainment in Monticello. You helped me out quite a bit with information on Monticello. I would encourage anyone who visits Monticello to please book a tour with Historic Monticello Ghost Tours, for you will enjoy the rich history, explore the town and so much more!

Jeana C., big thanks to you! I enjoyed learning from you about the Apalachicola Ice Company, as well as the Chapman Auditorium.

Royce R., thank you so much for providing me with the lovely photo of Jeana C., the Apalach Ghost Tour guide.

Mark C. Curenton, thank you for your efforts in helping me gather historical information within Franklin County.

Troy Snead, thanks for your comment on an article in *Southern Spirit Guide* regarding W.C. Reeder with the Old Calhoun County Jail.

Thank you, Waylon Moore, for your interview and story about Holmes Creek.

Thank you, Sarah McCoy, for your story about Holmes Creek.

Thank you, Brandon Young, for your interview and story about Saint Marks.

Thank you, Tyler Wilson, for your interview about the Waits Mansion.

Thank you, Frances White, for sharing your experience at the McFarlin House Bed and Breakfast.

Thank you, Rebecca Perry, for your personal interview and story related to Gadsden Fort.

Greg Byrd, thank you for your experience and for sharing the history of the Knott House.

Thank you, Randell Murph, for your interview and story.

Maria Martinez, thank you for your interview with me. I loved hearing about your experience at the Gregory House.

Thank you to all my friends, including my social media followers. I appreciate the constant interactions and seeing each of you get hyped for this book. I hope everyone enjoys reading this book, because I know I loved writing it! If you would like to support me on social media, feel free to follow me on all my socials at @authorkatlynjones, @mysteriesoftheunseen and on YouTube @lightinthedarknessasmr.

THIS BOOK IS PUBLISHED in memory of my late friend Elizabeth Pohler-Hewett, who passed away tragically on March 25, 2024. Thank you for believing in me as an author and as a friend. I loved the fact that we shared a love for the paranormal. Your love and positivity will forever be remembered by not only me but also so many others. I miss you so much. I love you. I hope I made you proud. This one is for you, sis.

PREFACE

What comes to mind when you hear about the region named the Florida Panhandle? Are you familiar with this area? Would you believe me if I told you that this region is more than just a popular place for tourism? The northwestern region of Florida has so much more to offer than just our white sandy beaches and bright blue waters. Although I do encourage everyone to enjoy our beaches, I would also like to encourage everyone who decides to read this book to dive into the Panhandle's history. This region has a wide variety of rich history that has yet to be fully discovered by not only many Florida natives but also people from all over the country. Each county has a multitude of cities that have plenty of stories just waiting to be heard.

As I dove deep into my research within the Panhandle, I honestly had no idea what I was going to discover. As someone who has lived in Florida for over twenty-five years, I am amazed by what I learned. Along with the history of each county, I was impressed to hear of all the ghostly legends and paranormal experiences found within the region. For me, as a paranormal investigator and true lover of anything supernatural, this book has truly brought a new perspective to the area with its hauntings. Some of these locations are well known, while others are just now willing to make themselves known.

As someone who has had a fascination with otherworldly happenings and ghostly legends, I wondered: How many locations in the Panhandle are haunted? I had my work cut out for me as I decided to take on a project within the Bible Belt. Many individuals in the South do not believe in ghosts and won't even entertain the thought of a place being haunted. But I am sure there are quite a few people out there who believe in ghosts as much as I do. Although there are plenty of known hauntings and tons of history throughout the Sunshine State, I genuinely believe that there is always more to be discovered. If you are seeking a thrill or even a different outlook on the northwestern region of Florida, I encourage you to stay tuned in as I dive into each county in the Panhandle.

Chapter 1
Jefferson County

1872 DENHAM INN B&B
555 WEST PALMER MILL ROAD
MONTICELLO, FLORIDA 32344

Which small town in Florida would you consider the most haunted? If you happened to guess the city of Monticello, you guessed right. Along the east side of northwest Florida is Jefferson County. Yes, this county was indeed named after Thomas Jefferson, the third president of the United States. Monticello was named after Jefferson's primary plantation, located in Charlottesville, Virginia. The city courthouse in Monticello was inspired by Jefferson's plantation. The commander of the First Florida Infantry Regiment during the American Civil War was James Patton Anderson, who lived in Monticello. Many locals believe that the county is haunted due to it being built on top of ancient Native American burial grounds, or it could be that the city intersects with three ley lines. Ley lines are straight alignments that run from one place to another. These types of lines are usually crisscrossed and hold a huge amount of energy. Where they intersect, some people believe that more paranormal phenomena occur. Either way, this generates a lot of energy that constantly flows through this city.

John Denham was a wealthy businessman. During the Civil War, most businesses were shut down, leaving many men with no way of providing for their families. John took his business and decided to align it with the

1872 Denham Inn B&B in Monticello, Florida. *Courtesy of Gary Yordon.*

Confederate army. It was his mission to keep them well stocked with supplies. It is said by many locals that Denham's favorite place to sit each night was in the cupola of his home. He quite enjoyed keeping an eye on everything so he could remain on top of his business. According to Michael Blain with Historic Monticello Ghost Tours, there is plenty of history and many spooky experiences to be shared while on the walking tour. Michael says that one participant had the opportunity to go into the cupola to sit in John Denham's chair. When this individual sat down, she immediately heard a crash so loud that she fell right out of the seat, causing her sunglasses to go flying. She never could find her sunglasses, and as she made her way down the stairs, she saw that two large portraits had fallen off the wall. This lady was convinced Mr. Denham didn't like her sitting in his chair.

Many different sounds can be heard while exploring or staying at the Denham Inn, like footsteps going up and down the stairs near the cupola and roaming freely around downstairs in the wee hours. Disembodied voices can be heard from any room at any time. A shadow figure of a man who is presumed to be Mr. Denham can sometimes be seen standing in the cupola just before sunset if you stand out in the front yard. Sometimes he can be seen in guests' photographs. Cold spots can be felt at random, and each room has a different feeling to it.

The most haunted and most popular room is the Blue Room, which is where John's aunt Sarah lived and died. Some say she still resides here. Aunt Sarah is quite fond of women and children. The Blue Room, specifically, is where her presence can be experienced and felt. Some guests have had encounters during their stay with someone they believe is Aunt Sarah. Multiple women have felt someone almost tucking them in for bed or felt as if someone was sitting or lying next to them as they were dozing off to sleep. Infants and children have also been tucked into bed, while other children have claimed to have seen an apparition of a lady speaking to them just before bed. People have seen the rocking chair moving with no one in it. The television is often turned on and off randomly as well. The lady who can be seen running in a white wedding dress in the yard is, in fact, Aunt Sarah.

YouTuber Hunting the Dead, while visiting with his family, captured multiple electronic voice phenomena, or EVPs, throughout the home, yes and no responses with dowsing rods and voices coming through the spirit box when he found a creepy doll in the bathroom closet. His family even experienced Aunt Sarah herself tucking his children into bed that night. He claims most bed-and-breakfast inns are welcoming and positively haunted.

USA Today states that the Denham home is the second-most haunted place to sleep with a ghost. If you are up for that type of challenge or are interested in investigating this home, please reach out to the innkeeper, Pat Inmon, to see what she can do for you.

MONTICELLO OPERA HOUSE
185 WEST WASHINGTON STREET
MONTICELLO, FLORIDA 32344

Near the center of the city of Monticello, Florida, is the Monticello Opera House. It was built in 1890 and was formerly known as the Perkins Block, after John H. Perkins. Perkins was a prominent businessman in the city for many years. Before this building was a theater, the first floor was previously used as a general store, a farm implement supply store, a sewing shop and a hardware store; the town post office was even located here at one point. There is a large foyer located on the second floor. It is the largest stage in the region, and people boast about its unparalleled acoustics.

Monticello Opera House in the 1970s.
Courtesy of Florida Memory.

Around the 1970s, the opera house could very well have been destroyed. Thankfully, a group of Monticello citizens decided to help save and preserve a part of history. The funds were put together in hopes of restoring this building to its new life, and it remains standing today. The building hosts musicals, straight plays and even some comical performances that draw people from all over. Along with singing, acting and laughter, there is much more that can be seen and heard around the Monticello Opera House.

According to a *Gainesville Sun* article, this Romanesque Revival–style building still holds its former owner, John Perkins, close. Locals say that Mr. Perkins can be seen roaming throughout the building. In an article in *Tallahassee Magazine*, executive director Michael Herrin says that Dr. Perkins usually sits to the stage left of the orchestra pit in the box seat. A small, spooky black figure can be seen by the window in the backstage ladies' dressing room. The usual adrenaline-type thrills occur here within the building: random bangs, lights going on and off and things moving out of the corner of your eye.

In a personal interview, a former performer named Nathaniel Williams told me that he had a frightful moment at the opera house one evening. It was roughly the year 2017 when he experienced his first apparition of a ghostly figure in the audience. The part that caught him off guard was when he was attempting to rehearse lines onstage before the crowds came in. The only thing that was strange for Nathaniel was that he was the only person onstage, and no one was supposed to be in the audience—but as he delivered his lines for the third time, he happened to look toward the back row, and there he saw a man watching the show. Totally caught off guard by the presence of a man he did not recognize, Nathaniel continued with his lines. When he finished his performance, the man could be heard applauding Nathaniel from the back row. Thankful for the man's applause, Nathaniel quickly made his way down to the man, only to find his body slowly evaporating from the seat of his chair. Scared and flat-out spooked, Nathaniel ran to find a friend to tell them about what he had just experienced. Many members of the opera house are unsure who this individual was, but some say it very well could have been Mr. Perkins enjoying the performance.

Whether you're up for an intriguing performance or whether you'd like to find a ghostly visitor sitting alongside you during the show, the Monticello Opera House is the place to be. If you are interested in learning more about the historical aspects of the building and would like to look around, feel free to contact the opera house directly for a tour.

PALMER HOUSE
625 PALMER MILL ROAD
MONTICELLO, FLORIDA 32344

Monticello is a town full of haunted locations. Many locals would consider this next place the most haunted location throughout the whole town. This house is highly active with spirits, and not many individuals can stay in or near it for too long due to its alarming and unexplainable activity. Many locals feel that the energy of the mysterious Palmer House is inviting. As some people visit the home, through either the Historic Monticello Ghost Tour or a personal invite from the current owner, Mrs. Jackie, they may experience a hair-raising or spine-chilling type of feeling coming over their body. Mrs. Jackie did turn the home into a place to hold her antique collection. Some have speculated that this could be the reason for the activity. This place has a way of drawing you in and wanting you to learn more about it.

This historic home was listed in the National Register of Historic Places on November 21, 1978. It was built around 1867 or 1868 by Dr. Thomas Martin Palmer. Dr. Palmer served the Confederacy during the Civil War as surgeon general. According to an article on Anomalien.com, Thomas's son, Dabney Palmer, is supposedly the person responsible for the alleged

Palmer House in Monticello, Florida. *Courtesy of Florida Memory.*

paranormal phenomena that happens in the home. Dabney followed in his father's footsteps and was known for being the town doctor and pharmacist. He typically worked out of the small office at the front of the property. This office is where he treated his patients; the morgue was located on the second story of his home. Dr. Palmer not only embalmed deceased patients, but it is rumored that he would also take their blood and pour it over their bodies while they were in the grave. It's unclear why he did this. Locals have rumored that Dr. Palmer did experiments on the bodies before burial. There was, at one point, a bloodstained wall that remained a mystery in the house. The blood would never truly disappear despite many efforts to remove it. Eventually, the entire wall was replaced. During the days of Dr. Palmer, there was a breakout of malaria. Palmer

Elixir 666 was invented to cure malaria by Dr. Dabney Palmer. *Author photo.*

was the person who created Elixir 666, which was used to treat this disease. Many individuals were cured thanks to Dr. Palmer's invention.

Some of the paranormal phenomena that occur at this location are the disembodied voices of people who are presumed to be former patients, as well as staff members of Dr. Palmer. A lot of the activity that occurs here is believed to be connected to the antique items stored on-site and even the entity of Mr. Palmer himself. Multiple people have seen the misty, see-through shape of a man in 1800s attire carrying a medical bag roaming throughout the home. People who have visited the home and even Mrs. Jackie herself have heard footsteps walking about. Many guests on the ghost tour have claimed to see a figure standing in an upstairs window. There is a haunted Victorian china doll with its neck snapped in half that's said to be full of an unusual energy. This doll is in an upstairs room near the front of the house. The odd thing about this doll is that no one can truly determine its facial expression, as it can almost be seen changing right before your eyes. It is said that this is the main reason the team from the Syfy TV series *Haunted Collector* could not stay a full night here. The team just up and left due to their purely horrifying experience with this doll.

If you have enjoyed reading about this location, I would encourage you to visit. If you are up for more of a historical and ghostly-type tour of the home, as well as seeing many more haunted places around the town of Monticello, I strongly recommend reaching out to Historic Monticello Ghost Tours next time you are in the South's most haunted small town. Come experience history while exploring these haunted locations, all while hearing the stories of the paranormal. Who knows; you just might experience the haunt of a lifetime!

CHAPTER 2
LEON COUNTY

**KNOTT HOUSE
301 EAST PARK AVENUE
TALLAHASSEE, FLORIDA 32301**

Imagine traveling through Florida's capital city, Tallahassee. What part of its history sticks out to you the most? Is it the roaring crowds at the Doak Campbell Stadium when the Florida State Seminoles win a game? The Old City Cemetery, which brings people from all over to see the tombstone of the "white witch" Bessie? Or is it the Florida Historic Capitol Museum that can be seen as you drive through the middle of the city? Some, while exploring the city of Tallahassee, will come across a historic home that holds quite a bit of history. In fact, the Emancipation Proclamation was first read on May 20, 1865, on its front steps.

According to an article from Visit Tallahassee, Florida emancipated the enslaved a month before the rest of the nation did on June 19, 1865. Roughly four million were freed by the Emancipation Proclamation throughout the nation. Each year on May 20, a celebration is held at the Knott House Museum, where the Emancipation Proclamation is read like it was in 1865. Also in 1865, the home was used as a temporary headquarters for Union brigadier general Edward M. McCook and his men. McCook was the official person to read the Emancipation Proclamation and announce the freedom of all enslaved persons within the region of Tallahassee.

Knott House in Tallahassee, Florida.
Courtesy of Florida Memory.

The county of Leon was named for Spanish explorer Juan Ponce de León. In 1824, Leon became a county. Leon County is known for being one of the largest producers of cotton in all the South. Apalachee Creeks and Seminole Native Americans resided around what is considered Tallahassee today for nearly ten thousand years. It was the Spaniards who thought that this area would be a great place to put the state capital, as it had plenty of resources to help things flourish. The state capital would also be used as a meeting point for western and eastern Florida to come together.

The Knott House was built in 1843 by a freedman builder named George Proctor for a former state official named William Knott and his wife, Luella. In 1928, the home was restored in hopes of turning into a museum. This hope would become a reality when the home was converted into a gallery. In 1997, the gallery was converted into the Museum of Florida History. Today, it is in the National Register of Historic Places.

A multitude of people believe that due to the home's history, there are numerous reasons why this place could be considered haunted. One Tallahassee native named Greg Byrd has experienced a fair share of haunts in the Knott House. Greg is a historian and paranormal investigator who instantly fell in love with this Greek Revival home. While visiting the home one day, he talked with the owner to see if he could potentially do an overnight paranormal investigation. Accompanied by two staff members, Greg set up his equipment and began investigating. At first, there were knocks and footsteps. One of the main things that stood out during the investigation was how friendly the vibe felt within this home. Not once did Greg fear that he should not be there. A man's voice came through the spirit box saying, "Welcome, Greg." In awe of how intelligent this male spirit was, Greg asked with whom he was speaking. It abruptly said, "Knott." On wrapping up his investigation, Greg came downstairs to find the lights flickering and the front door slowly opening. Everyone else who was in the building was upstairs.

According to another article from Visit Tallahassee, an employee of the museum took a photograph while she was working alone in the building and later discovered that, in the photo, there was a strange figure. This photo can be seen in the museum, as it is displayed with all the other collections that can be viewed. Some mornings, workers, on arriving to open the museum, find the house unlocked and the front door wide open. The staff ensures that the doors are locked at the end of each closing shift, so the fact that the door seems to open on its own is quite peculiar. Locals in the area claim to have seen the lights on and people moving around between rooms outside of normal business hours. Most of the staff who work at this museum can vouch for the fact that this place is, indeed, haunted but will be the first to tell you to have no fear; only friendly ghosts live here. If you would like to visit this museum for a bit of history or even a friendly ghost experience, feel free to check out its website for tour hours. The Knott House Museum does not disappoint.

THE WARRIOR ON THE RIVER
9330 WEST TENNESSEE STREET
TALLAHASSEE, FLORIDA 32304

Ever wanted to enjoy a secluded music venue and bar? Well, you can in Tallahassee, Florida. The Warrior on the River is located by the Ochlockonee River on West Tennessee Street. In 1961, it was known as the Confederate Inn; it later became the Confederate Supper Club. Around the 1980s, it was the Moose Club restaurant for a time. In 1992, it became Bell Bottoms, a music venue that supported country music. There were shootings that took place outside of the venue. Around 2007, everything about this building was going downhill. Everything was failing, and the owners had no luck in renting this location to anyone.

Many previous tenants used and abused this building and did not see its full potential until its current owners, Chris Goodwin and his partner, Alicia Kilman, rescued it. Their mission for this location is to create not only a music venue but also a place where at-risk youth can learn about anything within the music industry for free. Together, these owners want to bring hope to not only their community but also throughout their building by creating a more positive environment than previous owners and tenants. While there is positivity that flows throughout the building and land, there is still some eerie residual energy that lives here.

The Warrior on the River bar and music venue in Tallahassee, Florida. *Author photo.*

TikToker Chaz C.C.M.P. (@chazofthedead) claims that this location is known to have paranormal hauntings as well as some Bigfoot sightings throughout the grounds. There are more accounts of paranormal activity reported here than at other haunted locations throughout the Panhandle. The most haunted hot spot can be found in the upstairs office. The building sits above the Ochlockonee River, and people claim it is a gold mine for Bigfoot sightings. Wails, loud knocks and even running can be heard nearby. The venue hosted the North Florida Paracon in 2022, where paranormal teams and squatchers (people who believe in Bigfoot) gathered for a massive investigation. According to Stacy Brown Jr., in a video of him in Warrior on the River, he had a spine-chilling experience with his girlfriend while investigating one night. During a spirit box session, multiple voices came through. Someone by the name of Beth came through several times. A noise was heard in the other room; then "Quit that" came through the radio, and it stopped on the station 91.1. It was said at least once that someone needed help and that they were injured. Do you think it's a coincidence that the radio stopped on 91.1? Could these be victims of the shooting that took place here years ago?

One evening after an eventful night at the music venue and bar, Randall Murph experienced what he believed to be a group of sasquatches. He decided to step outside for a smoke and wandered around the side of the building to get away from the noise for a moment. Randall was thirty feet from the woods when he heard a yell that sounded nonhuman, along with shuffling footsteps. It was not until he started following the sounds with his eyes that he saw three sets of glowing yellowish eyes peering through the trees at him. The only way Randall knew how to describe the feeling was that he knew he was being preyed on. He knew if he moved too fast or too slow, something would happen to him. As he stood there, a group of friends came running out hollering at him, telling him to get back in there because he was next up for drinks. Randall felt like had it not been for his loud friends yelling and coming toward him, something could have happened to him that night. This was an experience he could never forget. He encourages anyone who enjoys a fun time listening to music while eating some tasty food and having drinks galore to please do their business at the Warrior on the River—but beware of the sasquatches, as this is also their land. Be entertained by this secluded venue, as the fun never stops here. Who knows what might happen if you do decide to show up. A Bigfoot or the spirit of a long-lost soul may try to reach you.

CHAPTER 3

WAKULLA COUNTY

EDWARD BALL WAKULLA SPRINGS LODGE
465 WAKULLA PARK DRIVE
WAKULLA SPRINGS, FLORIDA 32327

Most who live near the Big Bend of Florida are aware of what this part of the county brings as far as legends and the paranormal go. For the people who are unfamiliar, allow me to introduce you to the county of Wakulla. Wakulla County was founded on March 11, 1843. *Wakulla*, a word of Native American origin, means "mysterious waters." Wakulla is known for its important places in history, such as Fort San Marcos, Saint Marks Lighthouse and Edward Ball Wakulla Springs State Park. The Native Americans who resided within this county were mainly Apalachee. All through the county, there are burial mounds and shell middens. The Native Americans made what is now known as Edward Ball Wakulla Springs State Park a huge part of their home for many years. Many lived and died here, and some can still be seen on this land. If you look closely enough and are willing to open yourself up a bit, you might be surprised at what you find. According to Penny Lane, she has seen shadows of Native Americans early in the morning, just as the fog is low enough on the spring waters. Some locals even claim to have heard faint chants and even cries that can be heard all throughout the state park.

The swimming area in Edward Ball Wakulla Springs State Park. *Author photo.*

Edward Ball Wakulla Springs State Park holds one of the most alluring springs that can be seen in the state of Florida. Some locals believe that a legend called Wakulla Volcano tells the story of how this spring system came to be. Along with this captivating spring, we also have a one-of-a-kind lodge, Edward Ball Wakulla Springs Lodge. This hotel was designed in the Mediterranean Revival style. It was built by businessman Edward Ball in 1937. If you visit the lodge, be sure to stop by the gift shop and parlor, as it holds one of the largest marble bars in the world, a whopping seventy feet, three inches long. You may be familiar with the films *Tarzan's Secret Treasure* from 1941, by Richard Thorpe; *Creature from the Black Lagoon* by director Jack Arnold; and *The Waiting* by F.C. Rabbath—they were all filmed in this state park.

Many guests who have stayed in this very hotel have stated that this place is, in fact, haunted. Multiple individuals have claimed to have seen the giant stuffed alligator named Old Joe moving through its glass case around certain times. Old Joe was one of the biggest and oldest alligators around, and he was found in Wakulla Springs. He was just over eleven feet

Edward Ball Wakulla Springs Lodge in Crawfordville, Florida. *Author photo.*

Alligator Old Joe in the lobby of the Edward Ball Wakulla Springs Lodge. *Author photo.*

long, weighed 650 pounds and was roughly two hundred years old. He died around 1966.

According to Youtuber Hauntings With David, this location is the most haunted hotel in Florida. David explains in his video that there are rumors about a little boy who knocks on people's doors, trying to get people to play with him. There are rumors that room 23 is the most active room in the lodge. David's presence elicited a lot of electromagnetic energy within the lodge.

Penny Lane, a former server and receptionist at the lodge, is a true believer in the spirits that reside in the hotel. As someone who has worked here for over two years, Penny has seen and heard quite a bit within these walls. Although she had not personally seen Mr. Ball himself, she has had numerous encounters with Ball's sister, Mrs. Jessie Dupont. Mrs. Dupont usually shows herself in a flowing white dress from a bygone era with her hair up in a loose, high bun. Penny has seen Mrs. Dupont in her peripheral vision, and the spirit has made herself known throughout the Cypress Room in the dining hall. Penny has no doubt in her mind that Mrs. Dupont and Mr. Ball reside here. Although neither of them died here, this was their happy place.

Mrs. Dupont did not like it when maintenance was painting the Cypress Room and pulled the paintings off the walls and all the furniture out of the room. She was very upset, whereas her normal energy is welcoming and calm. After Penny requested that things be returned to normal in the room, Mrs. Dupont's anger quickly subsided. Mr. Ball can be felt around and on the elevator. He usually comes with the smell of tobacco. Most staff have noticed poltergeist activity—for instance, finding chairs in strange formations. Mrs. Dupont and Mr. Ball like to mess around with the chairs, almost making it a game with the staff members. Guests around here may experience unexplainable activity inside or outside of rooms 101 and 102, as those are Mrs. Dupont and Mr. Ball's rooms; they will make themselves known to people who are staying in their rooms.

Penny stated in an interview that a paranormal team once came through and got an EVP in the library of a voice saying the name Jacob, which is interesting. The team came down to Penny and told her what they got, and she told the team to go to the parlor and talk to the guy at the bar and tell him the name that was said. Coincidentally enough, the guy's name is Jacob.

Regardless of what you may have heard about Edward Ball, he did what he thought was right by creating this lodge and even did everything he could to protect it. On his death, he even freely gave the lodge and springs to the state in hopes of it being preserved. Some may say his fencing up part of the river was terrible in nature. But if it wasn't for that barrier of protection for the river, we wouldn't have the last two untouched miles remaining in the county today. I believe that is special, even if it was done for the wrong reasons.

There is a tremendous amount of history here, and I believe that sometimes diving deep into historical research is best done when you can step inside the location itself. Whether you enjoy a refreshing dip in the sixty-nine-degree spring water that stays that temperature all year long, take a tour on a boat throughout the spring or investigate the haunted lodge, I'd encourage anyone willing to visit to do a deep dive into the history of this place. Who knows, you may even see something unexplainable in the forest of Wakulla Springs State Park, like several park rangers have.

SAINT MARKS LIGHTHOUSE
1255 LIGHTHOUSE ROAD
CRAWFORDVILLE, FLORIDA 32327

Twenty miles southeast of Wakulla Springs, we have the Saint Marks Lighthouse, located in the Saint Marks National Wildlife Refuge. The lighthouse was built in 1831 with stone and brick and is estimated to be around eighty-two feet tall. The first tower was built in 1831, while the second tower was built in 1842. In 1835, the lighthouse keeper Samuel Crosby oversaw the Saint Marks Lighthouse. Crosby caught wind of the Second Seminole War and learned that other lighthouses were being attacked. He feared for not only his life but also his family's. He decided to write to the proper authorities to request extra protection for the lighthouse. Luckily for them, Saint Marks Lighthouse was not chosen to be attacked during this war. This lighthouse had survived natural disasters, such as the hurricane of September 1843. This hurricane caused a great deal of damage to the town of Saint Marks, and it even destroyed the town of Port Leon. Around October 2013, the United States Fish and Wildlife Service took over ownership of this lighthouse from the coast guard. Many often wonder what makes this lighthouse so special. This lighthouse is, in fact, the second-oldest lighthouse in Florida.

As you enter the Saint Marks Wildlife Refuge, surrounding the roads are roughly sixty-eight thousand acres of nothing but nature and wildlife. There is nothing but life surrounding you as you travel through this park. As you travel down the main road to the lighthouse, you will wonder how long it will be until you reach it, but I promise you, the wait is worth it. Once you are greeted with this lively place, it will only excite you more as you get closer to the lighthouse.

This lighthouse has had so much history within it and around it, and some visitors and even locals have experienced wild occurrences around and near the lighthouse. Locals and guests have heard footsteps in the lighthouse and in the living quarters. Many believe this to be the previous lighthouse keepers continuing with their daily duties. Some individuals have heard cries for help from within these thousands of acres. According to a placard in the park, on July 30, 1944, there was a fatal B-17 crash. There were thirteen B-17s from the 325th Bomber Squadron that left Avon Park Army Airfield. They were performing a mock-bombing exercise when a sudden thunderstorm caused the group to separate. One of the planes, unfortunately, had failures and broke up into several parts. Tragically, nine men lost their lives; a man named Private Marvin J. Magee was the only survivor. Magee wandered through the swamps for hours in the heat of the summer looking for help. He finally found someone on a horse and got a ride to the Saint Marks Lighthouse, which had a coast guard station.

Avid hiker and explorer Brandon Young experienced something that still gives him goosebumps as he tells his story around campfires today. After finishing part of his hike just before sunset, he started setting up his tent and sleeping gear for the night. After cooking a nutritious meal full of protein, he decided to clean up his mess and continue putting wood on the fire to keep it going during the night for warmth. Brandon got into his tent and began dozing off, listening to the wildlife in the distance. It wasn't long before he was out like a light. Sometime later, unsure of the time and startled by a loud crashing sound, Brandon frantically awoke. Grabbing a flashlight and his shoes, he stumbled out of his tent, looking for what caused that crashing sound. Unaware of the history of this location, he wandered a little ways from his camping spot, only to hear a man's voice in the distance saying, "Help! Somebody! Anybody, help!" Offering help, Brandon said, "I can't see you, but I've got a camp going, and I may not have a lot, but I will do what I can. I have some food and a warm fire." He waited for what seemed like forever, and no one ever walked over to him, so he went back to his tent. Just as he was dozing off, he heard the man's voice outside his tent saying, "Hello, you offered help to me earlier. Is the offer still available?" As he unzipped his tent, Brandon excitedly responded, "Yeah, man. Anything I have is yours if you need it." As he went outside the tent, he was stunned

Saint Marks Lighthouse
in Saint Marks, Florida.
Courtesy of Florida Memory.

to find that, once again, he was all alone. He began wondering if his mind was truly playing tricks on him or if someone genuinely needed his help. It wasn't until Brandon returned home and did some research that he found out about the crash that took place in the park. Brandon wants everyone to know that because the tragic event occurred in such a beautiful place, he truly feels that the spirits of those who lost their lives couldn't have ended up in a more gorgeous location.

There are many rumors about the activity in this location, and I truly think that where there is history to be found, there is always something lurking. I'll let you decide if this location is full of negative or positive activity. Either way, I promise you won't regret seeing the second-oldest lighthouse in all of Florida.

CHAPTER 4
GADSDEN COUNTY

QUINCY LEAF THEATER
118 EAST WASHINGTON STREET
QUINCY, FLORIDA 32351

What do Coca-Cola, shade tobacco and Fuller's earth have in common? Well, I'll tell you! Gadsden County is the home for all three of these products. Located on the northern Florida-Georgia line to the east of Leon County is Gadsden. This county became the Sunshine State's fifth on June 24, 1823. The county was named after a man who served in the First Seminole War and the War of 1812 alongside Andrew Jackson: James Gadsden.

One of the oldest and most prominent industries in the county is the shade tobacco industry. For those who are unaware of what shade tobacco is, it is quite literally tobacco plants planted with shady coverings put overtop of them. Originally, the only states to grow shade tobacco were Florida and Georgia. Eventually, the industry branched out to the state of Connecticut, where shade tobacco is now grown as well. The only Florida counties to grow shade tobacco are Gadsden and Madison. In the nineteenth century, Gadsden County produced a great deal of Fuller's earth. Fuller's earth is a type of clay that some locals like to refer as the county's "kitty litter." Most individuals liked to use this product for bleaching and cleaning cloth, as well as other items. Surprisingly, in the beginning of the twentieth century, bottling Coca-Cola became another large industry within the county. Locals

Leaf Theater. *Author photo.*

claim that the Coca-Cola stock is responsible for generating wealth in the community. Rumors state that a multitude of millionaires lived within the county for a long time.

Located on East Washington Street in Quincy, Florida, is the Leaf Theater. The Leaf Theater was built in 1949, and its grand opening was marshalled by the famous western singer and actor Roy Rogers. By 1980, the theater had shut down. The Quincy Music Group had decided to bring life to it in the early 1980s. The group can still be seen there today, hosting musicals. This musical group has experienced paranormal happenings inside the theater. A former projectionist by the name of Mr. McDaniel has been seen in the audience, mostly in the front row. The theater is known for footsteps being heard in otherwise complete silence, giggles from the audience while groups are rehearsing, disembodied voices and the overwhelming feeling of paranoia that can encompass the people who choose to visit this alluring place.

An anonymous commenter on the website floridahauntedhouses.com described an eerie experience she had one evening while she was visiting the theater with a friend. It was 2007 when she decided to watch a friend rehearse a version of *Fiddler on the Roof.* She was given permission to watch from the balcony. It was a tremendous view, as she could see the entirety of the stage from this part of the theater. When the show was a third of the way through, this person heard someone rattling a doorknob that was on the outside wall. This was an unexpected occurrence and really spooked the attendee, which prompted the guest to further investigate the sound.

As I made my way to open it, I noticed a steel bar bolted across the threshold and a chain from the doorknob to a bracket on the wall. Deciding to talk to the other person, I briefly told them that I couldn't let them in, as the door was sealed and I was unable to open it. The activity stopped, and I returned to my seat but couldn't help but feel bad [because] I couldn't help them. No joke, this happened at least three to four more times during the rest of the show. It was quite distracting, and I honestly thought it was someone playing a joke on me, since I was told that this place was haunted.

At the end of the show, I made my way back downstairs and approached my friends laughing, telling them, "You got me! The joke was funny." After the strange looks I received, I explained what had happened to me while I was upstairs. Every single person there froze, each of their eyes got big and even a few mouths opened. The stage manager finally confessed that there was no physical way possible for any person to get to that staircase, as it had collapsed over thirty years ago. He said two people had been killed in the fall. My skin crawled for weeks after this experience and the explanations had been told. What an insane experience!

One Youtuber by the username of handsupimhappy commented on a video about the theater, stating that they do costumes for musicals. Many times while working at the theater, lugging large boxes of costumes throughout the building, they feel they have been gently guided down the stairs by an unseen force. Hearing and feeling things you can't explain is common in the Leaf Theater.

If you are in the mood for a musical or a show, or even a behind-the-scenes look at the Leaf Theater, I dare you to contact the theater for more information on shows, tours and more.

McFARLIN HOUSE
305 EAST KING STREET
QUINCY, FLORIDA 32351

On East King Street in Quincy, Florida, is the one and only McFarlin House Bed and Breakfast. In 1895, this four-story Queen Anne home was built by a prominent tobacco farmer named John Lee McFarlin. Mr. McFarlin was a businessman who enjoyed wealth and particularly liked to entertain. Some homes and doctors' "offices" over a hundred years ago had a carriage port that homeowners, servants and visitors could use to arrive and leave by carriage or buggy. This home still has its carriage port attached today. Around the 1940s, the Lester family purchased the home. They decided to install a slate roof, which later helped preserve the home from further damage as the years passed. The McFarlin House was added to the National Register of Historic Places on December 27, 1974.

In 1994, Richard and Tina Fauble purchased the home. They saw potential in this home and wanted to bring it back to its former glory. All sides of Richard's family came together, all four generations of them, to build what is known today as the McFarlin House Bed and Breakfast. That dream became a reality.

Along with beauty can come pain and sorrow. Many people have said that this place is not haunted, but those who have stayed here sing a different tune. While the inn gives off a positive and pleasant vibe, there is a darkness that lurks within these walls.

According to Frances White, she is one of the lucky individuals who experienced something chilling one evening during her stay in the McFarlin House. She was staying in one of the rooms on the second story that evening

McFarlin House in the 1900s. *Courtesy of Florida Memory.*

when everything happened. Based on what Frances said, it was truly a rough night for her. She hardly got any sleep due to thunderstorms. Finally, just as she was able to get to sleep, she had a dream. In this dream, she kept seeing a farmer, someone she had never seen before. The strangest feeling Frances had came when she saw him just staring at her, as if he had a message or something for her. A loud clap of thunder woke her up, and standing in the corner of the room was the shadowy figure of a man. Suddenly, a bolt of lightning ripped through the sky, and this figure vanished into thin air. After this figure disappeared, there was the lingering smell of tobacco, as if it were drying. The smell lingered for almost fifteen seconds before fading. After that, there wasn't much sleep for Frances, as she was kept awake wondering who that figure was and what it was doing in her room. She mentioned it briefly to the innkeepers, and no one knew who she was referring to, but they made a guess, and the first person who came to mind was Mr. McFarlin himself. Other than that, who it could truly be is an ongoing mystery.

Paranormal investigators, come one, come all to figure out who this man could be. If you would like to stay at this beautiful bed-and-breakfast or enjoy investigations, contact the owners. Who knows what spirits are lurking around this over-one-hundred-year-old home. Is your team up for the challenge?

CHAPTER 5
FRANKLIN COUNTY

APALACHICOLA ICE COMPANY
247 WATER STREET
APALACHICOLA, FLORIDA 32320

To the east of Gulf County, Florida, is a county named Franklin. Some of the cities and towns throughout this county are inland, while some are closer to shorelines and rivers. Many people, when they hear of Franklin County, Florida, think of the quaint city of Apalachicola, as it is the county seat. At one point in history, there were roughly forty thousand Native Americans residing in the area. Different types of fur and varieties of produce were commonly traded between the Spanish and the Natives. In 1832, Franklin became a county. It was named after Benjamin Franklin. Most Florida counties are named after someone of importance. The county is known for its fishing and timber industries. For a lot of people in the area, these industries were their way of making a living and still are to this day. An interesting fact about the county is that during World War II, the U.S. Army used most of Franklin for training in the swamps and jungle-like environments. The training took place at Camp Jordan Johnston in Carabelle, Florida.

In 1831, the city of Apalachicola received its name. The state of Florida is known for having ports, which are ideal for importing and exporting goods, cotton, lumber and other materials. Imagine this: before railways were an existing way of bringing in goods, Apalachicola was the third-busiest port in the Gulf of Mexico. According to historian Dale Cox with Two Egg TV, one of the first things Confederate troops in Apalachicola did was make a battery of cannons along the coast to defend the port. On Saint Vincent Island, Port Mallory was built. Around 1862, the Confederates were told that they would have to leave Apalachicola. On leaving, they took their cannons with them. The Union navy, at one point, stated that it resided on this land, but the sailors never actually lived here; they just visited from time to time. As a matter of fact, the Confederate soldiers never really lived here either, but they spent a substantial amount of time on the grounds, so it was assumed that they did. Near the end of the Civil War, there was talk about bringing in the ironclad CSS *Jackson* down from Columbus, Georgia, on the Chattahoochee River along with

Portrait of Dr. John Gorrie, who invented the ice maker in Apalachicola, Florida. *Courtesy of Florida Memory*.

the gunboat CSS *Chattahoochee* and the torpedo boat *Viper*. Their mission was to break down the blockade, but the war ended, so they never got the chance to have that happen. In 1865, the *Jackson* and the *Chattahoochee* were burned to the waterline, and they sank to the bottom of the river. The Union navy ended up capturing the *Viper*. During an attempt to tow the *Viper* to Key West, it sank somewhere in the Gulf of Mexico. Brigadier General Alexander Asboth was the one to lead the Union troops here and then, later, up the Chipola River to the Battle of Marianna.

One part of history that is strong within Apalachicola happened with the help of a man named Dr. John Gorrie. Gorrie, who used William Cullen's refrigeration method from 1748, decided he wanted to help invent a machine to produce artificial ice, refrigeration and air-conditioning. It was his mission to help provide the best care for his patients, especially those who were fighting yellow fever. Using the principles of Dr. John Gorrie, the Apalachicola Ice Company was born in 1885. This business was quite successful, as it created a better way of living for most.

Original Apalachicola Ice Company in Apalachicola, Florida. *Courtesy of Florida Memory.*

A present-day photo of the Apalachicola Ice Company. *Author photo.*

On November 27, 1887, there was a freak accident: the ammonia boiler at the Apalachicola Ice Company failed, causing an explosion that blew up a small part of the building. Additionally, it took the life of one individual, Charles A. Glazier, who was the city commissioner at the time. The explosion also fatally wounded Captain William Moore of Columbus, Georgia. Because of the tragic event that took place, locals claim that this is the most haunted location in the city. Many souls have been seen roaming about the Apalachicola Ice Company. After the explosion, from around 1913 to 1922, renovations took place. Due to its overwhelming amount of debt, the company filed for bankruptcy around 1925. Today, only partial remnants of the original structure can still be seen along the waterfront on Water Street. It is frequently used for wedding venues and parties.

Jeana C. as your ghostly host with Apalach Ghost Tour in Apalachicola, Florida. *Courtesy of Royce R.*

According to Jeana C., who is a guide and partial owner of Apalach Ghost Tours, many spirits are very much still active and wandering the Apalachicola area. If you would like to learn more about the history and haunts surrounding Franklin County, I'd highly suggest booking an Apalach Ghost Tour in Apalachicola, Florida, where the haunts last all year long.

CHAPMAN AUDITORIUM
155 AVENUE E
APALACHICOLA, FLORIDA 32320

As people travel into the city of Apalachicola on Highway 98 each day, they may pass what they think is an ordinary auditorium for theater shows. Most people associate the haunts of Apalachicola with the Gibson Inn or the Coombs Inn, but surprisingly, the Chapman Auditorium is one of the more fascinating haunted locations in the county. In 1931, construction began on the cast stone auditorium. The building was to have an auditorium and eight classrooms. The progression of the building took much longer than expected. The Civil Works Administration ended up taking over construction during the Depression era. Eventually, the Federal Emergency Relief Administration resumed construction and, in 1934, completed it. The class of 1934 of Chapman High School was the first to graduate in the completed auditorium. The auditorium is one of the last few Art Deco buildings in the state of Florida.

The community theater group that holds productions at this location is called the Panhandle Players (PHP). In 1987, the group was founded. Jeana C., a native of Saint George Island, is a member of the board of directors and is also an actor with the Panhandle Players. Jeana spends quite a bit of time in the theater. She claims that two of the theater members have seen the same apparition of a short, stocky man in a white shirt from two different areas within the building: the lower-floor bathroom and by the light box. She had quite the experience when she was investigating with her boyfriend one night. The paranormal equipment that was used during the investigation was the Onvoy ghost app, dowsing rods, a Rem Pod and an EMF-detecting trip wire. These devices are used to directly communicate with the other side; they also help get clear messages relayed to paranormal investigators. Jeana's app had generated the words *specter*

Chapman Auditorium in Apalachicola, Florida. *Courtesy of Royce R.*

and *stairs*, so she looked at the closest set of stairs by the stage, and it was there she saw a black, wispy, static humanoid.

The second time Jeana investigated, she came back with friends, and they collectively heard their recently deceased friend state his name. This friend was someone who grew up and went to school with Jeana's boyfriend. He was also friends with many other PHP members. Once communication started, they asked him to try to communicate with the dowsing rods and the app. Their late friend continued communicating with the group by talking through the ghost app, saying that he didn't want to scare them. The group assured their ghostly friend that he wasn't scaring them and that it was comforting to hear his voice again. The friends ended up moving to another location within the building, and the device asked, "Are you sure I didn't scare you?" They then got hits from the EMF-detecting trip wire. Everyone was calm, and they never got scared. More than anything, they were just shocked at the direct communication happening right in front of them. The dowsing rod sessions were mainly held in the lobby near the bathroom, and that's where Jeana's friends first saw the physical form of their dear friend who had passed away. His presence appeared in the form of a mist, but based on his facial features, the group determined that it was him. Photos were taken of the stage that, on review, were found to have orbs present, but sadly, his apparition was not photographed. Jeana can confidently say that in all the time she has spent in this building, she never experienced anything until her dear friend passed away.

It is safe to say that this location is haunted by quite a friendly spirit. Although paranormal investigations are no longer allowed at this location, the building can be rented out if you can provide insurance. If you're interested in a great production, stick around for an outstanding show—or even just to look around at the beauty of this building. Who knows—our friendly spirit might just join you in the audience for the show.

TATE'S HELL STATE FOREST
290 AIRPORT ROAD
CARRABELLE, FLORIDA 32322

On scenic Highway 98 in Florida's Panhandle region, drivers will be met with breathtaking views of the Gulf of Mexico and eventually discover the world's smallest police station, which came to be on March 10, 1963.

Carrabelle police booth. *Courtesy of Florida Memory*.

This police station is in the city of Carabelle and looks like a phone booth. It has been featured on television shows and was even in a movie called *Tate's Hell*. You might be wondering what *Tate's Hell* is about. Well, I'm about to tell you how this movie got its name! While the city of Carabelle is known for its adorably tiny police station, the city itself is plagued by something much darker.

There is a particularly eerie wooded area that has acquired the name Tate's Hell State Forest. A multitude of individuals have said that the name itself is enough to send shivers down their spines. This location can be found roughly twenty-two miles east of Apalachicola, Florida. This state forest has a total acreage of 212,269, and while it may have a wide variety of compelling options for activities, it also has a fair share of ghostly inhabitants.

From the 1950s through the 1990s, part of the surrounding tree life that wasn't thriving was used to produce timber. Along with the abundance of land here, there are more than enough areas filled with marshes, streams, a bayou, sandhills, bogs and so much more, as well as an abundance of wildlife, such as bears, alligators, wildcats and countless others. The wildlife considered endangered or threatened here are the red-cockaded woodpecker and the gopher tortoise. A multitude of locals claim that this could very well be the ultimate environment for a sasquatch or a skunk ape to be lurking around. It was not until 1994 that the Florida Department of Forestry took over the wooded property.

Over the years, visitors from all over the world have traveled to the Sunshine State to spend their time in parks such as this one. While there is beauty to be found in Florida's state parks, there is also a questionable ambiance that can be felt pulsating throughout your being. Tate's Hell State Forest has a way of inviting the bravest of souls here to explore the most haunted forest in all of Florida. The legend goes that there is a swamp named Tate's Hell Swamp located within Franklin County that gives off one of the eeriest feelings to anyone who comes close by. Many locals believe this swamp is named after Jebediah Tate's only son, Cebe Tate. Jebediah married a woman of Cherokee descent roughly around the Civil War era. They decided to buy property in hopes of one day having a productive livestock farm. Cebe was born not too long after the war. For a long time, the family had the best of luck, with an abundance of livestock and production of food on their land. Due to unfortunate events, Jebediah lost his wife to scarlet fever; she died suddenly. From this point on, everything seemed to fall apart: the family, the land, their business. Curiosity got the best of Jebediah Tate, and he decided to pay a visit to a Native shaman to grasp a better understanding of everything and why his luck had taken a downward spiral. The shaman heard him out, and an agreement was made that each year, a pig would be brought to the shaman. Jebediah also promised to not enter the shaman's sanctified forest in exchange for prosperous farmland. The shaman made it clear that if this agreement between them was broken, Jebediah's family would be cursed. They each agreed, and things were great until Jebediah ultimately broke that agreement. He later died from malaria, and his son, Cebe, ended up paying the price for something his father agreed to. This string of bad luck and financial problems went on for years. Cebe eventually married a Jewish woman around 1875. One day, Cebe realized one of his cows had gone missing. As he made his way to the swamp along with his dogs, things felt different. Suddenly, his dogs ran after a panther that he didn't even see coming his way. It wasn't until later that he realized his dogs would never return. He decided to take a break from wandering around in this forest, so he sat down under a tree. He felt an electrifying *zing* on his leg, and looking down, he saw he had been bitten by some sort of venomous snake. He decided that he had to keep moving. Roughly seven days later, he stumbled across two men who were walking nearby and said, "I'm Cebe Tate, and I just came through hell." It wasn't long after this that he died. This legend has been passed down throughout the years. It is believed that if you go into the forest, a curse will be placed on you. It is believed that many who enter the forest do not escape unscathed. There have been numerous reports of people entering the forest and never coming out, and those who have come out have done so with serious injuries. The rotting smell of flesh has reportedly been detected in and around the forest grounds. Some locals have even claimed to have seen Tate trying to hitch a ride home around the hours of one to three o'clock in the morning. If you are up to getting the hell scared out of you, be sure to come by Tate's Hell State Forest and see what it's all about. But if something were to happen, you can't say I didn't warn you.

CHAPTER 6
LIBERTY COUNTY

FORT GADSDEN
SUMATRA, FLORIDA

Did you know that along the Apalachicola River lies one of the most haunted historic forts in Florida? Fort Gadsden has a past that not a lot of people may know about. Let's start out with a bit of background about the county in which the fort resides. Liberty County was named after the American ideal of liberty and was created in 1855. This county is, in fact, the smallest in the Sunshine State; it also had a population of eleven in 1857. Despite the county being so underpopulated, the fort itself is teeming with spirits. But first, let's go back to its tragic origins. In 1859, Bristol became the county seat.

According to Kathy Alexander with Legends of America, during the last days of Spanish Florida, a battle took place at Fort Gadsden. In the War of 1812, a British major named Nicholls was on a mission to recruit Seminole Native Americans and escaped Black slaves in Florida. It was his mission to get them to fight back against the United States. They eventually gained Prospect Bluff in 1814. Here, they offered freedom and land to the formerly enslaved. Many more were brought in from other states for the same freedom. In 1816, Major General Andrew Jackson gave orders to destroy the fort and lacked any form of empathy when sending the enslaved back to their racist and monstrous owners. A U.S. Navy gunboat on the Apalachicola River fired a cannon, which hit part of the fort. The explosion killed 270 people. Around

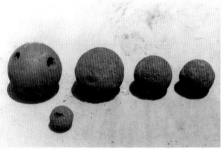

Left: Replica of Fort Gadsden in Sumatra, Florida. *Courtesy of Florida Memory*.

Above: Cannonballs from Fort Gadsden in Sumatra, Florida. *Courtesy of Florida Memory*.

1818, Jackson ordered Lieutenant James Gadsden to build a new fort on top of the old fort. This would be called Fort Gadsden. The Confederates ended up using the fort as their port, for the Apalachicola River provided an efficient shipping system for the importation and exportation of goods. The fort eventually was abandoned due to an outbreak of malaria. Approximately 2,000 people lost their lives, and their bodies are scattered about the property via a mass grave where the old fort was. With so much death on-site, many apparitions continue to wander the grounds of Fort Gadsden.

According to Two Egg TV, a barge crew told Dale Cox about what they saw one day while on the Apalachicola River. The crew saw a Native American and Black individual dressed in old-timey clothes standing there watching as they went by. According to Emerald Coast Paranormal Concepts (ECPC), they encountered someone they believed to be an antiquated carpenter who had worked for a prestigious company of that era. They found out this information by using an electromagnetic field detector, also known as an EMF meter, and by asking questions, to which the spirit would respond by interacting with the detector.

A Liberty County local, Rebecca Perry, decided one day to visit Fort Gadsden with her mother, Janet, who is a medium and quite in tune with the spiritual realm. On making the turn to enter the property, her mother shifted into "work" mode.

As we got closer to the fort, my mother told me she feels a type of loss come over her. She feels as though many people are surrounding her and that they are trying to tap into her energy at this very moment. Janet said, "We are here to help, and we mean you no disrespect or harm." Suddenly, there was a shift in the energy around us. The energy at first felt like we were intruding, and then it became more open and welcoming. My mother asked, "What is your story? What happened to you? Do you know you're dead?" At the time, we didn't bring any equipment; we just had our camera. As soon as I was about to restart the camera, we both audibly heard a voice next to us, questioning, "We're dead?" My mother felt the presence of a woman about childbearing age stepping forward, and she said, "Yes, you are. You don't have to remain in such a place. If you'd like, you can move on." We weren't expecting another response, but my mom got a vision of a woman and her baby being taken from her. Janet then stated, "If you had your baby taken from you, my condolences. I may not know what that was like for you, but my heart is with you. I love my children, and I couldn't imagine the pain you felt at that moment. I do feel as though your baby is at peace and is waiting for you in the light." The air temperature instantly changed to cold. It was honestly about twenty degrees cooler. About the time that we realized how cold it was getting, I felt someone hug me. My mom told me that the spirit of the lady said, "Thank you" to me and "Thanks for bringing your mom, Janet, here to give me peace." This encounter has stuck with me for years, as I've never had such a unique experience before.

Who knew a place that experienced some intriguing times in history could share these memories with those who visit its location? If you'd like to pay your respects to the site, check out the details online for more information.

GREGORY HOUSE
2576 NORTHWEST TORREYA PARK ROAD
BRISTOL, FLORIDA 32321

In Florida's Torreya State Park is a southern antebellum-style mansion by the name of Gregory House. Around the mid-1930s, Torreya State Park was established. The Gregory House was built in 1849 by a prominent Calhoun County planter named Jason Gregory. This house remains standing to this day but not without lots of help in restoration after many years of deterioration. As time went on, Gregory's home went to a downward spiral without being tended to for a long time. His daughter decided to restore it and bring back its full potential. Later, the home was donated, moved to the park and reconstructed. An interesting part of Torreya history is that in the early 1800s, during the first Seminole War, Andrew Jackson and his troops marched over the river to get to what is the state park today.

The hauntings surrounding this location are some that you might not think would happen, especially out in the middle of nowhere. According to a blog called *Cane Pancake Gravy*, a tour guide on the property said that, typically, people who are sensitive to certain energies can pick up on some of the vibes throughout this location. While the home was abandoned for a while, ladies of the night would visit and make this their meeting spot to engage in nefarious affairs with johns. One of the stories goes that one of the ladies got into a fight over cards and was murdered right in the middle of the staircase. After finding her body, park rangers would refuse to enter the house, even to change the smoke detector battery. A full-body apparition of a prostitute has been known to chase park rangers down the stairs and out of the house. Rangers have also heard infants wailing while alone in the building, and there is speculation that prostitutes would get pregnant from unprotected sex and wouldn't want to deal with the responsibility of being a parent. These ladies would murder their babies and bury them on-site, hoping that their carelessness would be nothing but a distant memory.

In Torreya State Park, there is an area that most do not know of that is another hot spot for hauntings. By day, this small blue waterfall has a way of captivating people from all around, including families, hikers and campers. Locals say that a white shadow can be seen hovering near the waterfall, whether it be in the daytime or the nighttime. Some individuals claim to have heard their names being called and have felt tingly soft whispers in their ears. The grounds are also home to a child who was murdered near the waterfall. Most believe the child is the white shadow that can be seen and heard on the grounds.

One visitor named Maria Martinez had an experience at Gregory House like none she'd ever had before. She decided one day, after work, just about an hour before sunset, to go on the last tour of the day at Gregory House. After the tour, the ranger on duty that day allowed Maria to walk throughout the house to look around. As she was walking downstairs, she heard cries of anguish coming from the second floor. She thought maybe the ranger was hurt upstairs, as she was nowhere to be found downstairs. As Maria went up the stairs, she found herself peering around a corner into one of

The Gregory House in Torreya State Park, Bristol, Florida. *Courtesy of Florida Memory.*

the bedrooms. To her surprise, she found an elderly woman wearing thick, runny makeup and a patterned beaded dress who seemed distraught. Maria, thinking this woman was some sort of volunteer, decided to slowly approach her and ask her if she was okay. As soon as the words left her mouth, the elderly woman's head moved up, and then her mouth dropped open and she said, "Welcome, Maria. I've been waiting for you." It was almost like the woman's mouth and voice were being controlled by a ventriloquist. Panic-stricken, Maria slowly backed away, with her eyes remaining on the lady, as she was mesmerized by what was right in front of her. As Maria was backing up to the threshold, this woman began to sob. The difference was that this time, the woman had blood-filled tears flowing down her cheeks along with her mascara. As the tears continued to flow, her cries got louder and louder, as if the whole house was filled with her pain. As soon as Maria got to the threshold, she felt a tap on her right shoulder. As she turned around, she saw the park ranger who gave her the tour advising her that the park was closing soon and they would have to close the house for the night. Maria was in disbelief about what she had experienced, but she claims the woman still haunts her in her dreams. She believes that this woman was a former madam associated with the prostitutes who were murdered in the house and is seeking revenge on those whom she believed killed her most lucrative women.

Come experience the haunts and history of Liberty County with a walk through Torreya State Park. Maybe you'll visit the Gregory House, where you may meet the tempestuous madam and her zombified ladies of the night. After all, according to William Congreve's *The Mourning Bride*, "Heaven has no rage like love to hatred turned, nor Hell a fury like a woman scorned."

CHAPTER 7
GULF COUNTY

**GULF COUNTY COURTHOUSE
1000 CECIL G. COSTIN SR. BOULEVARD
PORT SAINT JOE, FLORIDA 32456**

Like numerous Florida counties, this county, for a long time, survived on cotton production, railroads, ports and paper mills. This county has always had a way of bringing people from all over to visit its Gulf Coast. Port Saint Joe has been welcoming ships for over 150 years. Named after the Gulf of Mexico, Gulf County officially became a county in 1925. Around 1927, the first courthouse in Gulf County was built in Wewahitchka, Florida. Previously mentioned in the Wakulla County chapter are Mr. Edward Ball and his brother-in-law Alfred I. DuPont. Edward Ball was a businessman who thrived throughout the Florida Panhandle for many years. In 1933, Mr. DuPont bought the Apalachicola Northern Railroad. Mr. DuPont bought the railroad in hopes that it would eventually lead to the future success of a papermill in the city of Port Saint Joe. Unfortunately, before his dreams could become a reality, he passed away in 1935. Through a trust and wanting to fulfill Ball's brother-in-law's vision, the Saint Joe Paper Company was born. As a result, the Saint Joe Papermill was established to honor Mr. DuPont's legacy, opening its doors in 1938 and producing many jobs for local families. The paper mill ran for over sixty years before deciding to close its doors.

Gulf County Courthouse in Port Saint Joe, Florida. *Courtesy of Florida Memory.*

Later, in the 1960s, the new courthouse was built in Port Saint Joe. To this day, the Port Saint Joe Courthouse has remained standing, even through multiple tragic events. One of the most popular tragic events was Hurricane Michael in October 2018. This category 5 hurricane tore through not only Gulf County but also its sister county, Bay County. In both counties, some homes and commercial buildings were completely ripped down to their foundations. This was a horrific time for all the locals, including myself. For years, people struggled to get back on their feet. The county desperately tried to be patient in rebuilding and helping the community one step at a time.

Another gruesome event took place at the Port Saint Joe Courthouse: a shooting on Tuesday, July 28, 1987. Lives were changed this Tuesday morning after court let out. Three people died by gunfire from a man full of rage. The three people who tragically lost their lives were the lawyer Thomas B. Ingles; W.L. Bailey, the circuit judge; and Peggy White Paulk, who was a witness for her sister-in-law, Eleanor Inez Huckeba. Ingles was forty-three years old. He was a twice-wounded Vietnam veteran and a former assistant public defender. Bailey was sixty-four years old and a one-term state legislator as well as a longtime jurist.

Court began like any other event in Port Saint Joe that morning but ended in suffering. Lawyer Ingles had requested a hearing regarding Clyde Melvin being behind on his monthly alimony. Also called to court was Melvin's ex-wife Eleanor Inez Huckeba. When court ended, Melvin's anger grew tremendously, and he pulled out a six-shot .357 Magnum and a four-shot .22 caliber Derringer. At the time, there was no bailiff present. On a mission, he shot lawyer Ingles first, then Judge Bailey and, finally, Peggy. Then he ran after his ex-wife. Melvin, ironically enough, worked for the Port Saint Joe Paper Company as an armed security guard for roughly thirty years.

Most people claimed he never gave anyone problems and that he didn't seem like the type of person to react this way, other than that he was just a socially awkward guy in the community. Clyde Melvin was shot by Sheriff Harrison. He was charged with three counts of first-degree murder.

Jennifer Stanley stated in an interview that she believes the gruesome event may have left some souls lurking in or haunting this building. Staff claim that lights can be seen flashing on and off in the judge's quarters and that the elevator works erratically. Jennifer has heard disembodied voices and footsteps running on the catwalk that connects the courtroom to the jail. She has even seen shadow figures throughout the holding cells. Overall, most will tell you that this place has the most unsettling and heavy feeling to it, while other people will tell you that friendly spirits stay here. Would you feel brave enough to take the stand where all these murders occurred?

GULF CORRECTIONAL FACILITY
500 IKE STEELE ROAD
WEWAHITCHKA, FLORIDA 32465

Not commonly known to outsiders for its haunting activity is Gulf Correctional Institution of Wewahitchka, Florida. Opening its doors in 1992 was only the beginning of what was to come. Most prisoners will say this place is full of pain and suffering, but the guards will say there is more than meets the eye here. It is not uncommon for prisoners here to get into gruesome fights or even be found dead in their cells. Some days, some of the correctional officers even fear for their lives, as this is such a dangerous job.

One former correctional officer named Benjamin Wilburn was spooked on more than one occasion in this state prison. One night, Wilburn was working the night shift in the two-story confinement dorm. The cell to the left side was 101, and the cell to the right was 112. There were four shower cells next to the cell on the right. After the inmates finished their showers, they went to bed. The only lights on were the dorm lights and the shower cell lights. Benjamin sat down to do his paperwork for the night around two or three o'clock in the morning. As he silently did his paperwork, he began feeling a sense of worry and became on edge. Feeling full of anxiety and frozen in fear, he saw out of the corner of his eye a dark hovering mist coming from the depths of the dorms closest to him. This pitch-black mist

Gulf Correctional Institution. *Author photo.*

was shaped like a human form and could be seen coming out of one jail cell and gliding into another. After multiple attempts to figure out what could have caused this shadow figure, Wilburn decided to talk to his sergeant at the officer's station. Wilburn went to ask the sergeant if he knew anything about a dark mist that could be seen floating back and forth between jail cells. The sergeant simply stated nonchalantly, "Oh yeah, this place is haunted for sure," and claimed that this was common around that area of the institution. As they continued talking about the hauntings of the prison, they both saw in front of them the same mist that Wilburn had seen just moments prior. As soon as they both acknowledged its presence, it disappeared into thin air. Wilburn claims that, after the incident, this was a place he didn't want to remain in for too long at one time. He concluded by saying, "Imagine how we feel right now; imagine how the prisoners who have life sentences here feel. They must remain here within the jail, and that's terrifying."

According to correctional officer Tanner Brown, full moon nights seem to be the worst at the state prison. It was near midnight when Brown was doing a perimeter check. Along the outside of a building, he thought he saw another guard. As he got closer to the guard, he saw it had no human features on its face at all. As this figure approached Brown, Brown's heart rate went up. When it was less than five feet from him, the figure suddenly dropped to the ground and disappeared before his eyes.

Another incident happened in a dorm inside the prison. Brown heard what he thought was someone being violently attacked. He entered the dorm only to find no one there. Then the door slammed behind him. He quickly grabbed the door and got the hell out of there. Brown claims that these are two of the craziest experiences he has ever had working there.

A former captain of Gulf Correctional Institution wishes to remain anonymous. His experience at this institution was, hands down, one of the most horrifying of his life. During a round one evening, this captain was checking in on each of the inmates in confinement, moving from one dorm to another. As he got to the dorm closest to the end of the hall, he went to shine his flashlight into the window, and there he saw, on the bottom bunk, a man who looked like a creature straight out of a horror movie. This man was sitting in a low squat with his hands on the bed in front of him—sitting almost in the position of a cat. The most terrifying thing about all of this was that the man in the dorm had red eyes glaring back at the captain. As this captain walked away, he became curious about whether his eyes were playing tricks on him, so he decided to do a quick double take. On looking back into the cell with the light, he saw the man still sitting in a cat-like position. About a second later, this man shaped-shifted into a dark mass that abruptly pounced toward the door. Completely scared out of his mind, the captain ran out of confinement all the way back to the officer's station, where the nearest guards were located. Uncontrollably shaking, the captain reluctantly approached his superior. In a fit of stammers, he admitted why he wouldn't be completing the rest of his rounds that night. The humanoid figure with catlike tendencies is still believed to roam the prison. Would you dare to come face to face with him? If you wish to find out more about the hauntings here, I would ask a correctional officer or a staff member over doing hard time in this notorious state prison.

CHAPTER 8

CALHOUN COUNTY

OLD CALHOUN COUNTY JAIL
20830 NORTHEAST W.C. REEDER DRIVE
BLOUNTSTOWN, FLORIDA 32424

Florida has many highways that lead you on quite a wandering ride to places you have probably never been before. Luckily for Calhoun County, even if you are unfamiliar with this side of Florida, you cannot miss the city of Blountstown, as it is the centerfold of the county, and Highway 20 runs directly through the city. If you are looking for a more rural, scenic route, travel from the center of Blountstown to Highway 71 and take it north about eleven miles, and you will arrive at the rural town of Altha. Calhoun is popularly known for its farming industry, specifically food and cotton production. In 1838, Calhoun became a Florida county; it was named after John C. Calhoun. Calhoun was a United States senator from South Carolina. Blountstown was specially named for John Blount, who was a Seminole chief. General Andrew Jackson had this chief help guide him when it came time to invade Florida and claim it from the Spanish. The chief was awarded land for a reservation in 1823. For a while, the reservation thrived. Eventually, the government came through and decided to purchase the land and move the tribe to another state. It wasn't until around 1800 that the county seat became the city of Blountstown.

About three blocks east of the intersection of Main Street and Highway 20 is one of the county's most haunted locations. According to Glenn Kimbrel, who is a Calhoun County sheriff deputy, the old, two-story Calhoun County Jail has had its fair share of hauntings. Kimbrel's uncle George used to work for the department and would tell Kimbrel about all the things that would take place in this jail. One incident, in 1942, involved a male prisoner who was put in a cell by himself. The deputies could hear cries and pleas for help coming from the cells upstairs. As soon as the sheriff deputies got to the man, they were told to urgently check on the man who was alone in his cell. Deputies walked over to the cell only to find blood splattered everywhere and dripping off the ceiling. They found the man alone in his cell, dead in his bed. An odd discovery was made when the sheets were pulled back off his body: bite marks. These bite marks enveloped the entirety of the man's body. The discovery was a stunning experience for not only the prisoners but the deputies as well. Some chilling experiences cannot be fully explained. There were no leads about this incident and what could have caused it to happen. This haunting is still very much a mystery in this town. In previous years, around Halloween, the city has held haunted houses and spooky-themed events at the old jail. Some, as they faced their fears in this haunted jail, were not prepared to see, in real time, the blood pouring from the ceiling onto the cell floor.

According to a comment by Troy Snead on the blog *Southern Spirit Guide*, his great-uncle was W.C. Reeder. Troy says he remembers visiting the old jail when he was young. According to a family story, in the 1950s, Reeder arrested a woman who had been caught prostituting herself. As he began locking her up in her cell, a man showed up out of nowhere. Locals speculated that this was her pimp, as he told W.C., "I'm here to get my woman." W.C. insisted that the man go back downstairs. Refusing to listen, the man pulled a knife, which led W.C. to shoot him.

Old Calhoun County Jail in Blountstown, Florida. *Courtesy of Florida Memory*.

Another individual who wishes to remain anonymous had an experience at this jail. This story, which has been passed down from generation to generation in his family, is about his great-grandfather, who was put in jail for something he did not actually do. As the story goes, the guy's great-grandpa was working in the fields one day when a sheriff rolled up with his gun drawn, demanding he come with him. In utter confusion, the man dropped his plow and quickly threw up both his hands in the air. He asked the sheriff if he did something wrong. The sheriff quickly ran to him, tackled the man to the ground and then cuffed him. The man, now lying face down on the ground, was covered in fresh dirt and struggling to get a word in. He made many attempts to get the words out: "You got the wrong guy." Feeling hopeless, the man cooperated and willingly went with the sheriff to the jail. After being interrogated for what felt like forever, the man was finally told what he was being charged with: murder in the first degree. Allegedly, he had murdered a sheriff's deputy who was actively working during that time. He sat in jail for years before anyone ever thought of giving his case a look— until there was an emergency evacuation one evening due to a murder-suicide that had taken place in the jail. The family believes this story lines up withthe timeframe of Kimbrel's uncle George's story. The contained men's cases were being investigated. It turns out that, in the end, the only evidence that the sheriff had was that this guy's great-grandpa was innocent. The terror that the men in the jail felt when witnessing the murder that night could confirm that there was in fact something malevolent at play in the Calhoun County Jail. The murder was so gruesome it was as if the prisoner was possessed by the Devil himself. While the jail is no longer standing, it's understandable why the men of this time have avoided it like the plague.

Although the old Calhoun County Jail has been torn down, some locals and even prisoners from the new jail claim to have heard faint cries and bloodcurdling screams from the grounds on which the old jail resided. The local rumor is that even if the building is no longer present, the energy that was once there can still be felt—especially close to Halloween.

CHAPTER 9

JACKSON COUNTY

JOSEPH W. RUSS JR. HOUSE
4318 WEST LAFAYETTE STREET
MARIANNA, FLORIDA 32446

Located on the northwestern border of Florida is Jackson County. This county was founded on August 12, 1822, and was named after America's seventh president, Andrew Jackson. In the War of 1812, Jackson served as a general. In 1821, he also served for approximately six months as Florida's first military governor. As time went on, the county formed multiple towns. The first town was established in January 1821 and was called Webbville. In September 1821, Marianna was founded by a Scottish native named Robert Beveridge.

During the Civil War, a bloody battle took place. The Battle of Marianna took place on September 27, 1864, between the Union and the Confederates. The Union commander was Brigadier General Alexander S. Asboth, and the Confederate commander was Colonel Alexander B. Montgomery. The Union had eight killed, nineteen wounded and ten missing or captured. The Confederates had ten killed, sixteen wounded and forty-one missing or captured. Some even considered this battle "Florida's Alamo."

The front yard of today's Jackson County Visitor Center is right where the Battle of Marianna took place. The building in which the visitor center resides is also known as the Russ House. The Russ House is located at

Front of the Joseph W. Russ Jr. House in Marianna, Florida. *Author photo.*

4318 West Lafayette Street in Marianna, Florida. This historic house was built by Joseph W. Russ Jr. from 1892 to 1895. Russ built this residence for himself and his mother, Mary Beman Russ. Only two years after he built the house, Joseph Jr.'s mother, Mary, passed away. Joseph married Bettie Erwin Philips in 1899. A year later, they welcomed their little girl named Frances Phillips Russ, later known throughout the town as "Big Mama."

Over the years, the house has gone through different architectural changes. Two porches were added on. One of the porches was on the main/ground floor and the other on the second-story level. Each porch created a circle, almost giving a half-moon shape to the house. Frances's mother, Bettie, was diagnosed with a malignancy in 1925. Joseph, in search of answers to save his beloved wife's life, took her to every nearby hospital to get her the help she needed. Unfortunately, there was not much that could be done, and Bettie passed away about six months later.

Four months following his wife's death, Joseph married his second wife, Wilma "Willie" Treadwell Russ. Willie was known as a gold digger because she married Joseph for his money. Three months after their wedding, due to the Crash of 1929, Joseph lost all his money. This hardship caused Joseph Washington Russ Jr. to take his own life by putting a firearm to his temple and pulling the trigger. Frances was the one to discover her father lying in a pool of blood and lifeless, as she was the one who initially heard the gunshot. The State of Florida decided that since it had only been three months since the wedding, the bride would receive half of the estate, and the other half was Frances's. Others claim that Frances had bought out Willie's other half of the property. At this time, Willie and Frances were swimming in debt, but Frances was taking it a lot harder. Overwhelmed in her grief and overflowing debts, Frances continued to do everything in her power to keep her beloved home. She sold the land surrounding the house just to pay the lien that was put on the property by the city. Frances obtained a second mortgage so that her children could pursue college. Eventually, the estate was added to the U.S. National Register of Historic Places on July 18, 1938. The Russ House had five generations of family living there for many years.

There is no doubt about it: the Russ House has paranormal activity. Paranormal and research team Emerald Coast Paranormal Concepts, also known as ECPC, has had many years' worth of experience here. This team has dedicated thirteen years to paranormal investigation and research. Founder Tracy Todd and his wife, Susan Todd, cofounder of the team, have had many experiences that could cause any skeptic or nonbeliever to jump with pure fear. They have been investigating the Russ House for roughly ten years. Not only have they dedicated their time to research toward finding out the truth, but they have also thought logically and scientifically while remaining unbiased in their research. Tracy Todd and his ECPC team have experienced multiple paranormal phenomena at this location. They have heard footsteps walking around throughout the house and up the stairs leading to the second floor. There has been music playing while the team was sitting in complete silence. There have been phantom smells, such as lavender, alcohol and tobacco. The team's audio recording devices have captured multiple types of voices coming through, such as those of men, women and children. There is no doubt about it: these spirits are comfortable with this team. Susan claims that people who have investigated with them have experienced a tightness in their chest in the parlor. A coincidence? Willie suffered and died from lung disease. Some have claimed to have seen her, while others have felt her presence. One thing is for sure: do not go down into the parlor and call Willie a gold digger, as it in fact does upset her. One of the ways people have acknowledged her presence is by scent: she reeks of lavender.

One individual named Mckenzie Hill experienced what she believes to have been Joseph's second wife in the parlor. Mckenzie was visiting with family when she got a tour of the estate. As she was being shown the oldest (and still functioning) pocket door, she started to smell the scent of lavender. At first, it was not strong; then after about a minute, it grew to become extremely potent. She began looking around to see if there was a wall plug going, but she saw nothing of the sort. The lady giving the tour took notice of the confused look on her face and said, "Is everything OK?" Mckenzie, looking baffled, replied, "I looked everywhere to see if there was a wall plug or anything that could have this smell, but I smell lavender, and I feel not myself right now." The tour guide replied, "Oh, I see you have met Willie. We call her 'lavender' because that is the smell she presents to us when she is down here." Mckenzie's mother also had an experience in the parlor. She felt like someone was sitting next to her on the couch. As quickly as Mckenzie's mother looked beside her, the tour guide said, "She truly is making herself known to your family. She must like you." The family all smiled and continued with the tour. The Russ House has many stories; whether they be about ghosts or history, I will leave that up to you.

BELLAMY BRIDGE
4057 BELLAMY BRIDGE HERITAGE TRAIL
MARIANNA, FLORIDA 32446

Imagine driving down a winding county road only to find out that you are passing one of Florida's oldest steel—and most haunted—bridges. About ten miles outside the city of Marianna, located off Highway 162, you will find

Bellamy Bridge Heritage Trail. This trail will lead you down a wandering half mile to the infamously haunted Bellamy Bridge. The first bridge was built in 1840, while the latest bridge, which was made of steel, was built in 1914. This bridge still exists today, but much to the dismay of Floridians, it is impassable due to deterioration. Many people from all over the United States come to see what is left of this once-enchanting steel frame. Some who visit claim that it is not the living that they must fear there.

Many ghostly legends are about a lady in white roaming around looking for a lost soul she once loved. This legend happens to be about a lady in white, but she differs from most, as it was her wedding day when she was supposedly burned alive. The newlyweds were named Samuel and Elizabeth Bellamy. They both were so madly in love that they never feared it would one day end. Elizabeth was scorched alive when the corner of her wedding dress became engulfed in flames from a candle burning nearby. Some claim that she ran down to the waterline of Bellamy Bridge to extinguish the burning flames on her raw, weeping wounds. Others, in their version of this story, claim that she ran onto the bridge and jumped for her life. Some say that the flames were extinguished, and it was days later that she passed away due to an infection from her wounds. No matter which version of this story you may

Bellamy Bridge in Marianna, Florida. *Courtesy of photographer Jacob Whitfield.*

hear, it all can be considered quite a tragedy. As the bride was considered dead, her lover, Samuel, was left to deal with her loss alone. He mourned the loss of Elizabeth, and some even say that he drove himself mad until he chose to end his life. People have said Elizabeth still lurks around the bridge in her wedding dress, looking for her long-lost love.

The Bellamy Bridge Heritage Trail contains more than just this haunting; it has land full of blood, sweat and tears. Speaking of tears, this trail also contains a huge section of the Trail of Tears. For those who are not familiar with the Trail of Tears, it was a gruesome time for the Native Americans of the East Coast. Some Natives were tempted with promises of land and freedom on the West Coast if they signed away their property. Most who survived found out that this was all just a bunch of broken promises and a way for the government to take charge. This journey from east to west was so brutal that only one-fourth of the Cherokees were left after all was said and done. The Cherokees were not the only tribe who embarked on this journey of terror. Some other Native American tribes that were included were the Creeks, Chickasaws, Choctaws and Seminoles. Innocent men, women and even children died trying to survive. The ones who were not willing to sign over their land were forced to leave against their will. All this negative energy and emotions of dread, rage or even sadness left a paranormal imprint around the Bellamy Bridge Heritage Trail.

Another interesting event that took place near Bellamy Bridge was the Battle of the Upper Chipola. This battle took place on March 13, 1818, on Florida's Upper Chipola River. It was one of the most important battles of the First Seminole War. According to local historian Dale Cox's book *The Ghost of Bellamy Bridge: Ten Stories of Ghosts & Monsters from Jackson County, Florida*, two more tragedies took place on this trail. One incident happened due to a dispute among a group of moonshiners by the names of Dan Smith, Sylvester Hart and Levi Hart. The men were cousins. They were each involved in making and selling illegal alcohol. One night, Dan saw that a bunch of alcohol had gone missing, while the rest of it had been wasted on the ground. Dan and Levi had their suspicions about who had done this. On May 9, 1914, Levi killed his cousin Sylvester with a pistol.

The second incident was another cold-blooded murder. In this case, we have a husband who was upset and fighting with his wife. She decided that she was going to leave him, and she wanted to take the child as well. The husband then took his daughter, and they went for a ride in their wagon to the trail by the Bellamy Bridge. He then took out an axe and decapitated his little girl. He then proceeded to use the blade of the same axe to slash his own throat. No one knows how long their bodies were left there, but they were discovered by people passing by, and to this day there are no records of this case available at the coroner's office.

Due to all this history being so close to Bellamy Bridge and even the continuously flowing, spring-fed Chipola River, one can only imagine how much energy is presented there. Emerald Coast Paranormal Concepts (ECPC) has been investigating this bridge for almost ten years and can confirm that this location is a hot spot for activity. Susan Todd, cofounder of ECPC, has stated that before Hurricane Michael, there was a bit of activity around the bridge, but since the hurricane, things have amped up. The whole atmosphere has changed there. Todd also explained in an interview that while running an investigation with people from all over, she would ask the group to stop when they got to part of the trail that felt different or uneasy. She continued to say that over 80 percent of these people would stop at the same location on this trail. There is no documented reason for this unexplained phenomenon. ECPC mentioned that at one point, they encountered an individual who had crashed and died on a nearby road, but there is no documentation available about this occurrence.

At this location, individuals have experienced hearing a woman crying out for help. Her wails can be heard echoing off the flowing water surrounding the bridge. They have witnessed a woman who could be considered Elizabeth in the form of a floating, misty apparition appearing before them and disappearing just as quickly. Some have even said they have seen a scalded face contorted in anguish and despair, forever roaming and lost, looking for her long-lost love. Others have felt a chill running down their spine as they hiked down this thrill-seeking trail.

In an interview, Carl Pence told me about his experiences along the trail and at the bridge. He stated that as he was walking the trail with family, he felt a sense of being watched. He felt uneasy, almost as if something was hunting him down. He felt this on the way back from the bridge to the parking lot. He had brought his own equipment, and it was fully charged. When he and his family were at the posts of the bridge, as he stood there in awe taking in the sight of this magnificent steel structure, he noticed that all his equipment, including his phone, had died. He muttered to himself, "That's weird. I know I charged these fully." His daughter Emma, standing next to him, heard someone speaking to her. She frantically looked around, wondering who was there. Carl checked the whole area for about ten minutes, ensuring the safety of his family. Everything was clear. Carl claims that he still is unsure about what they came across, but he says he would encourage everyone who enjoys a thrill to give this location a shot.

Now that you've heard the history of this place and a little bit about the experiences that have been had here, I would like to shed some light on what local historian Dale Cox states he feels is necessary for people to know: the truth about the infamous hauntings at the Bellamy Bridge. As the legend goes, Elizabeth died from a fire; this is false. Elizabeth is said to have had died of fever on May 11, 1837. Her eighteen-month-old son also passed away a short seven days later from the same cause of death as his mother. As for Samuel Bellamy, he didn't take his own life until sixteen years after the death of his beloved wife and son. He died from a straight razor that he took to his throat while staying in a hotel. The legend of Elizabeth Bellamy came about due to an author by the name of Caroline Hentz, who wrote the book series titled *Marcus Warland: Or, the Long Moss Spring*. People assumed the book was about Jackson County, since Hentz lived her last two years of life in the area. Some would say this book was all about a plantation in Georgia, just as some will continue to believe in the ghostly legends and hauntings of one of the oldest bridges in Florida.

CHAPTER 10

WASHINGTON COUNTY

WASHINGTON CHURCH
2191 OWENS POND ROAD
CHIPLEY, FLORIDA, 32428

One thing is certain about this location: there is history, and the land is infiltrated with residual energy. For years, locals have reported strange happenings and unexplainable activity. You may be wondering why that is. Allow me to elaborate on the history so that you can better understand why there may be things still lurking around some years later.

In 1825, the Florida county named Washington was established. This county was, in fact, named after the first president of the United States, George Washington. George Washington's Virginia home was in Mount Vernon. Around the 1800s, railroads helped give a boost to the economy within this area of Florida. In 1882, a man named William Dudley Chipley, who was a railroad pioneer, became the founder of the town known today as Chipley. Vernon was originally the first county seat, but later, the town of Chipley decided that with the railroads arriving, it would be more fitting if the county seat were changed to Chipley. In 1927, this took effect. This county eventually developed more cities to produce more forestry industries.

In Washington County, Florida, there is a church by the name of Washington Primitive Baptist Church that was established in 1848. This church is also known as Hard Labor Church. In 1932, the original church

Washington County Church in Chipley, Florida. *Author photo.*

was replaced, and the church remains standing over ninety years later. Many people may have not heard of this location, although I know some have. In 1864, the Battle of Vernon took place just outside of Washington Church. When I say outside of the church, I do mean the battle literally took place on the road next to the church. This battle took place only one day after the Battle of Marianna. Some of the Union soldiers who fought in the Battle of Marianna also fought in this skirmish. Captain W.B. Jones caught wind of the Battle of Marianna and made the decision to help his neighboring county. On September 28, 1864, the Union and the Confederates would, yet again, come face to face with each other. They collided by complete accident and began fighting right on the road next to Washington Church.

Brigadier General Alexander S. Asboth, who had fought in the Battle of Marianna, ordered Captain Jones and his men to leave, claiming that this wasn't a battle the Confederates would win. According to legend, Private Stephen Pierce, who was a part of Company H of the Fourth Florida Infantry, was the one who stood there in the middle of this battle on the dirt road, taunting the Union soldiers. Some believe it was an act of bravery, while others think it was foolish. As you can imagine, the Union soldiers were not incredibly happy with this movement made by Pierce, and they chose to open fire at what was left of the Confederates. Captain Jones quickly realized that his men were outnumbered and they would have to either run or fight with everything they had

Stephen Pierce's grave in Hard Labor Creek Cemetery, Chipley, Florida. *Author photo.*

within them. The Confederates chose to stay and fight back. Many of the soldiers were taken prisoner, and some eventually escaped. The Battle of Vernon was an intriguing one. One man lost his life, while others were wounded. Stephen Pierce was fatally wounded in this skirmish. Due to his wounds, Pierce passed away, and he was buried next to Hard Labor Creek Church in the cemetery.

Hard Labor Creek not only has a church and a cemetery, but there is also a little bridge that many have claimed is haunted. All the legends surrounding this location are enough to send chills down anyone's back. In an interview, Christopher Johnson stated that he has experienced several diverse types of encounters. One night, he was driving through but suddenly got the feeling he was being watched, so he stopped his vehicle. He felt as if something did not want him there, almost as if he was invading someone's space. He turned to his left, toward one of the parts of the cemetery, and he saw a man in the distance walking over to his truck. At first glance, this man looked like a farmer, but as he got closer, Christopher said, the gentleman looked like a soldier. In complete disbelief, Christopher shrugged off the fact that he thought it was a soldier. As the man got within about five feet of him, Christopher realized that this *was* a soldier, and he was dripping in blood, crying out for help, as his hand covered up a wound. Completely freaked out but intrigued, Johnson asked the man if he was injured, only to be surprised by his reply: "Help,

Bridge where the spirit of a woman in white can be seen by Washington Church in Chipley, Florida. *Author photo.*

I've been shot!" After this remarkable response, the man walked away and started to disappear into thin air. Christopher believes he might have had an encounter with one of the soldiers, or it could have very well been Mr. Pierce himself.

In an interview, Whitney and Oliver Marks shared a frightening experience they had one night at Hard Labor Creek. The couple has always been told by locals and family members: whatever you do, do not go to Hard Labor Creek Church unless you want to see some scary things. Not believing the legends, the couple decided to visit the church there, just to see if something would show itself to them. As they pulled up to the church, they realized that something didn't quite feel right. Sound familiar? They both pushed past that feeling of uncertainty and pulled their vehicle up to the front of the church. One after the other, they got out of the car and began to walk up to the church's front door. As they walked, Oliver saw a shadow run past the window to the right of the church. He immediately said, "Whitney! I saw a shadow figure!" Whitney quickly responded, "Yeah, right," and then laughed. As soon as the words left her mouth, she saw a woman staring out the left church window. This woman seemed a bit angry that they were there. Startled, Whitney took a step backward and fell. Oliver looked at Whitney and said, "What happened? Are you all right?" Confused and stumbling over her words, she replied, "I—I—I saw a woman in the window staring at me. I thought it was my reflection. She scared the hell out of me!" Oliver helped pick Whitney up, and they walked back to the car. As Oliver went to open the door for Whitney, he let out a big "Ah!" and jumped back. There was a lady sitting in Whitney's seat. Whitney looked in the car, only to see that same angry lady in white staring back at her. Feeling trapped, the couple just held each other and finally mustered up the courage to say, "We mean no disrespect. Leave us alone. Be gone." She vanished right before their eyes. As Oliver and Whitney drove down the road, they came across a small bridge and saw a young woman walking toward it. As they got closer, she turned toward them and began running to their car. It seemed as if she ran right through their car. As they drove through her, they felt deep sadness and dread. They thought to themselves that this woman must have gone through something horrific to be feeling this way. Locals rumored a woman had died by suicide there. If you see a woman walking on Hard Labor Road just before a bridge, she will either charge at your vehicle or even try to ask for a ride. Others claim that if you look in your rearview mirror, you just may see this lady sitting in your back seat, staring back at you. Would you be brave enough to visit or even drive through this haunted location?

WASHINGTON COUNTY NEWS
1364 NORTH RAILROAD AVENUE
CHIPLEY, FLORIDA 32428

What comes to mind when you imagine a haunted building? It is your typical eerie-looking building that makes your skin want to crawl with fear, or does it seem to fit right in with the other buildings in town? Imagine this: as you come into downtown Chipley, you will encounter one of the county's most haunted buildings. This building happens to be filled with workers who loved their jobs so much that they continue to linger, going about their daily routine.

Although obituaries are common in the newspaper business, so are articles reporting truth and spreading awareness. The *Washington County News* has been around for quite some time. To be exact, it's been here since 1893. I would like to dig a little deeper and tell you what this place has to offer as the most haunted location in the county.

The owner and editor for the *Washington County News* was Earl Sellers. According to Dorothy Pyfrom Odom with the Washington County Historical Society, Sellers initially started with his newspaper in a store named Little

Washington County News building in Chipley, Florida. *Author photo.*

Big Store, where he shared a space. In 1940, he decided that he would buy the building next door and establish the *Washington County News*. From the mid-1920s until the early 1960s, Sellers operated the local weekly. In 1964, he decided to sell his part of the paper to Dave Fleming.

This building is truly an incredible place for learning more about the past and present. Locals claim that this is no place to mess around with, as quite a few unexplained experiences have happened here. The staff of the news building have had more than enough jump scares. According to Dorothy Odom, the employees here have a little phrase that they like to use when they experience what they think is Mr. Sellers walking toward his old office from the back of the building to the front. That saying is: "Mr. Sellers came to work today."

Some people have experienced placing items in a certain area and then, when they reach for them, finding them gone; chairs being moved from one cubical to another; and filing cabinets being opened and files strewn everywhere when the cabinets were securely shut and locked. Editor of the *Washington News & Holmes County Advertiser* Jennifer Rich states that pens have flown off her desk. She once saw shadow figures inside the building while standing outside. Diane Moore, a reporter with the *Washington County News & Holmes County Advertiser*, stated that Mr. Sellers would knock things over and even turn off the lights.

The father-daughter duo who runs the YouTube channel Hiking the Haunts has had quite a bit of useful information regarding this location. The daughter even expressed at one point that she had an eerie experience. She felt compelled to tap on the glass front window of the building while saying, "Hey, mister." She instantly felt regretful, like she shouldn't have done this. It wasn't her intention to taunt, but she did think to herself, *Nothing could happen, right?* As soon as that thought rolled around in her mind, she heard a male's voice saying, "Hey," back.

According to YouTube commenter Moepejolresurrectionlife2451, "The Washington County News was haunted long before the death of Mr. Sellers. I published the paper for thirty-five years and I knew him well. The strange sound in the back, the unexplained occurrences and various people having that creepy feeling when I was in the back of building, have been going on since Sellers was alive."

Mr. Sellers still is legendary in death, as he was in life.

CHAPTER 11

HOLMES COUNTY

DOUBLE BRIDGE OF HOLMES CREEK
GRACEVILLE, FLORIDA 32440

As you travel Florida Highway 77, you will see multiple rural areas. Just shy of the city of Graceville lies a unique hiding spot for multiple hauntings in Holmes County. Few will pass by, and some will even ride through this location each day, but only a few know of this place and have experienced what the double bridge of Holmes Creek has to offer.

On January 8, 1848, Holmes was created as Florida's twenty-seventh county. Holmes is near the Florida-Alabama state line. The county's name is said to have been inspired by two prominent individuals in history, Native American Chief Holmes and North Carolinian settler Thomas J. Holmes. Chief Holmes settled here in the early 1800s. Lamentably, during the First Seminole War of 1818, Andrew Jackson had him killed. Thomas arrived here around 1830, approximately eighteen years prior to this newly discovered land being given its name. Over the years, this region of Florida has been well known for its lumber production. In the past, some of the lumber that was imported here was used for building one of its most haunted locations today.

Off Highway 77, turn onto Piano Road and follow this road until you reach Spruce Road, and then turn onto Spruce Road and follow until it turns into Woodham Road. On Woodham Road, when you turn, you are greeted by a desolate wooden double bridge. Underneath these barren bridges flows a transcendental creek. This creek is said by locals to give off a certain energy when one crosses over it or is in the vicinity of it. If you are looking at the location on the map, you'll see that at the beginning of the first bridge, to the east side of Woodham Road, is Jackson County, Florida. To the west of where the second bridge ends is Holmes County, Florida.

This location is filled with far more than just ghostly activities. The nature that surrounds this brook is a home for many skunk apes, also known as Bigfoot. One individual named Waylon Moore lived in the area for decades. Waylon finally had enough of all the activity surrounding his home and decided to relocate to a more comfortable setting. It wasn't uncommon for Waylon to hear loud knocks coming from outside, in the tree line, at nightfall. One evening, just about thirty minutes before sunset, he noticed that his dog Buck was missing from his backyard. Moore hollered to Buck for what seemed like forever, only to realize that maybe he ran down by the water. Concerned, Waylon headed down to the brook to search for his missing dog. As he approached the first bridge, he began frantically calling out to Buck. At first, he got no response, so he continued calling two more times. On calling out to his dog for the third time, he finally got a faint bark back and could hear his collar jingling in the distance. Right about the time the jingling of Buck's collar stopped, Waylon heard one of the deepest, most terrifying grumbles he had ever heard. Suddenly, the area became so quiet that he didn't know which way to turn. As Waylon stood there, overwhelmed by his fear, he felt a nudge on the back of his leg. Startled, he slowly turned around to find Buck, low to the ground, shaking profusely in a state of terror. Trying to muster up some sense of strength, he whispered, "Let's go home." As they began to move toward their home slowly and cautiously, they heard fast movement from behind them. They bolted home. As they arrived safely back inside, Buck began jumping with excitement as Waylon praised his good boy for a job well done.

Later that evening, Waylon and Buck were lying in a state of tranquility on the couch. They both enjoyed feeling the warmth of the cozy, crackling fire. Almost asleep, they both woke up to a loud thud on the back sliding door. Waylon grabbed the shotgun and did a thorough sweep of the house and the perimeter of his home. Everything was clear, so they ended up going to bed. Moore claims he has never had such a frightful chain of events happen to him in one night. This ultimately led him to relocate to a different part of the county in a less rural area. He says whoever resides in or visits the area should beware of the sasquatches.

Another individual named Sarah McCoy told me in an interview about her intriguing experience she and her friends had one night. Being locals to the area, they actively sought out a thrill-seeking and haunting experience. They had always heard the rumors about Holmes Creek, but they wanted to find out for themselves what all the hype was about. As they began making their way down the dirt road to get to the two bridges, Sarah said to her friends, "Are y'all feeling a bit uneasy?" They both agreed, saying, "Yeah, I almost feel like we shouldn't be here." All three of the friends kept walking, thinking maybe they were feeling this way due to it being dark and foggy out. Sarah thought to herself, *This darkness and fog could make anyone get spooked out easily, right?* The legend of Holmes Creek says that anyone willing to get close to the creek in the dead of the night will meet the green lady who floats limply in muddied brook.

As soon as the group of gals got to the first bridge, they heard a loud knock. Not knowing what that could be, they thought nothing more of it. As they sat down in a triangle on the wooden structure, everything became quiet. This was the quietest they had ever heard this area get. A little unnerved

Double Bridge on Holmes Creek in Graceville, Florida. *Author photo.*

but trying to remain calm, they began focusing their gaze on the creek. Something green off in the distance made each of them curious about what it could be. After a few moments, the green figure of a beautiful woman could be seen floating down the river, almost as if she was asleep. As soon as the gals looked over the edge of the wooden structure of the bridge, this peacefully resting green lady's body lunged out of the water so abruptly that the ladies fell onto their backs screaming. As they lay on their backs, this green lady's face changed to that of an older-looking hag. The frightening lady demanded to know what they were doing there. The three ladies, lying as still as can be, said nothing. Now with their eyes closed, they heard what sounded like a group of people swarming around them. Wishing they were anywhere but there, Sarah finally opened her eyes to look around, and nothing was there. Everything was calm. The crickets were chirping, and the sound of water flowing could be heard beneath them. They stood up, looked around and decided they wanted to be in the comfort of their shelter. None of the gals said anything on their walk back. When they arrived at Sarah's house, all three of them sat on the couch and questioned what had truly happened. Each one of them had a different experience with the green lady, and no one knows why. Sarah's message to anyone who thinks they might be willing to visit here is: be cautious, and don't come alone. They all feared that they wouldn't return home that night, but they feel extremely lucky that they did.

WAITS MANSION
209 WEST KANSAS AVENUE
BONIFAY, FLORIDA 32425

In Holmes County resides the city of Bonifay. Located around Kansas Avenue is a one-of-a-kind two-story Mediterranean Revival–style home known as the historic Waits Mansion. This home was built by a successful lumber company owner named George Orkney Waits. The mansion was built from 1919 to 1920 for Wait's wife, Harriet. James C. Waits, the son of the original owner, sold the mansion after his parents decided to relocate. The home went through multiple renovations, including being converted into a single home, then into apartments and then into a bed-and-breakfast. According to my research, this home is now privately owned and used as a private residence.

Waits Mansion. *Courtesy of photographer Jacob Whitfield.*

There have been multiple rumors for many years claiming that this mansion is haunted. Several people who have lived here and visited as guests have had rather unusual experiences. According to an article on Backpackerverse.com, the home is known for having an angelic spirit present. The story goes that a local teen named Donny made the rash decision that since that mansion was up for sale and he knew no one was living there, he would sneak into the home to see what it looked like up close and personal. Donny carefully and cautiously made his entrance into the home and began roaming around. He thought to himself that this place was a palace with such beauty, and he just knew he had to tell his girlfriend, Sandra, about it and bring her by. Later that night, he talked to Sandra, and they set up a time to visit the home the next night. Then they each said good night and went to bed.

That night, Donny had the weirdest dream he'd ever had. He knew that at the bottom of the staircase to the left, there should have been a large living area. But all he saw was this white-cloaked figure with no face floating, watching him. The odd thing is, it looked right at Donny and said, "This is where pain comes for her." He jolted awake, only to see the morning light peering into his bedroom window. *Good, it was only a dream,* he thought.

The next night, Donny and Sandra entered the mansion. They decided to explore. Donny saw what he described as a type of aura; he didn't feel anything negative. He heard a voice that said, "You see as you are." This was a scary experience for him. Sandra, on the other hand, wasn't so lucky. Totally terrified, Donny said, "Sandra, we need to leave." He found Sandra in a corner quivering with terror, tears running down her face. Donny was unsure what she saw, but it had to have been bad, because she freaked out as he approached her and fell down the stairs. She was holding her leg as if she had injured it. Donny ended up carrying her out of the house and driving her to her home outside of Bonifay. He never knew what had happened to her that night, as she never spoke to him again after he dropped her off at her home. All he knows is that whatever is there still lingers, waiting for the next set of visitors to arrive.

Another experience with the Waits Mansion is from Tyler Wilson. During an interview, Tyler stated that he was staying in the mansion when it was a bed-and-breakfast. He had an unusual but comforting experience. His wife had recently split up with him, and he needed to find a place where he could unwind—although "unwinding" also meant contemplating suicide. He wanted to get away and get his thoughts together while staying there. One hot summer night during his stay, he was lying in bed with a mind full of racing thoughts. As he lay there, it felt as if something cold came in and lay right next to him. At first, the cold was very worrisome, and then after a minute, Tyler felt nothing but love surrounding him. Imagine something cold on the outside but warm on the inside; this is what it felt like. It felt as if someone was surrounding Tyler with love and comfort during a frantic time in his life. At this point, he knew that ending his life wasn't the right path for him anymore. Tyler felt like something had saved him that night. All his depression and sadness had been taken from him. The next morning, as he woke up, he decided to call his wife and rekindle his relationship with her. After a few months, they were back together again, stronger than ever. Tyler felt whatever was there that night was there to help protect him and surround him with white light. He doesn't know what it was to this day, but he claims it sure helped save his life and his marriage. He is extremely grateful.

Overall, there is no doubt that this location is haunted. If you feel that this location is worth visiting, please reach out to the property owners, as this is a private residence and their home. It would be considered trespassing if you decided to venture there of your own accord.

CHAPTER 12
BAY COUNTY

CASTLE DRACULA
12390 FRONT BEACH ROAD
PANAMA CITY BEACH, FLORIDA 32407

Most people come to visit Florida's white, sandy beaches and bright blue, tranquil waters. Some may be curious about what it might be like to stay here and wonder what else they can discover. I can assure you that the beach is not the only thing that Bay County, Florida, has to offer. While Bay County is notorious for making spring break a wild adventure for college students, some might remember this county for its sandy beaches that could go on for miles without a building in sight. Some may even remember the family fun attractions, such as Miracle Strip Amusement Park, Goofy Golf, Castle Dracula, Shipwreck Island Waterpark and many more. While some of these attractions no longer exist, I believe there is fun for every age group here. Some visitors may prefer a relaxing day at the beach to soak up some rays and even take a dip in the warm water. If you are the curious type regarding history or even the paranormal, I encourage you to stick around as I discuss my home county with you.

In the northwestern region of Florida is Bay County. In the 1820s, the main area for early settlers was the Saint Andrews area. Saint Andrews is where a lot of our county's success started. In the 1860s, salt production was booming in this area. The Confederates did everything they could to make

Original salt pot used during the Civil War in Bay County, Florida, located on Beach Drive. *Author photo.*

it successful. Salt production thrived so much that many people flooded the area, willing to fight for a piece of it—which leads us to the Saint Andrews Skirmish. This skirmish took place on March 20, 1863, when the Union and Confederate soldiers fought on Beach Drive. The soldiers from each side fought with everything within them, but it wasn't enough for the Union to win this battle, as the Confederates greatly outnumbered them. As time went on, the bay grew with the success of a port, which created more opportunities for the county. This county was founded on April 24, 1913. Bay is combined with portions of other counties, including Walton, Washington, and Calhoun. On July 1, 1913, there was a celebration for the new county.

Not only is Bay County dear to me, but Saint Andrews also holds a special place in my heart, as my family was here for many generations dating back to the 1800s. In fact, my family played a small part in Bay County's history. In November 1934, a harbor pilot by the name of Graydon York helped guide the first large vessel, *Maiden Creek*, captained by a Mr. Reed, through the old pass. This harbor pilot wasn't just anybody to me: this was my great-grandfather.

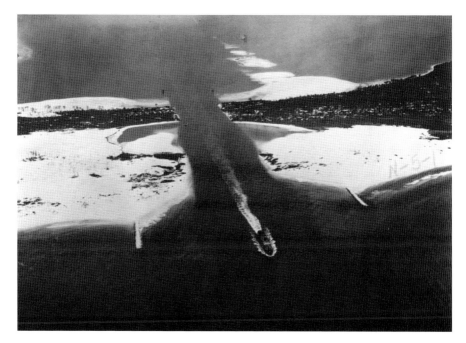

Author Katlyn Jones's great-grandfather Graydon York, a harbor pilot, guiding the *Maiden Creek* through the pass in Bay County, Florida. *Courtesy of the Bay County Library.*

In remembrance of the popular attractions on Panama City Beach, Florida, we have Castle Dracula. Some might recall this being a wax museum, while some believe this location was full of terror. Some individuals' screams could even be heard from outside its walls. Around the summer of 1976, Castle Dracula opened its foreboding doors for business. Many were brave and faced their fears in each room that lay ahead of them, while others never even made it to the entrance. The ones who were strong enough found themselves walking or even running down the winding hallways to get to the next room. According to locals, this so-called wax museum was far from having any wax at all. Many will say Frankenstein was the main appeal of the attraction. Everyone who visited desired to get a picture with him. As rumor has it, Castle Dracula mysteriously burnt down in the summer of 1987. No one really knows why or what really happened.

One local, Mike Smith, genuinely believed that this location was haunted. He claimed that the energy radiating from within the séance room set the mood for the entire place. Mike remembers one day walking through those infamous winding halls with his little brother Sean. As they approached each room, they felt a different vibe. They both excitedly left their parents behind as they made their way to the séance room. As they approached this room, they immediately felt a cold and tingly sensation running throughout their bodies. The teenage brothers looked at each other, and Sean asked, "You feel that?" Mike replied, "Yeah. Something doesn't feel quite right here." Sean was eager to stay a little longer, and Mike was eager to move on. They both went silent, just listening, taking everything in. Suddenly, they heard a woman calling out to them, saying, "Boys, come closer." As the guys looked around for a female presence, they saw no one. Apparently, their parents had walked outside to get some fresh air while the guys enjoyed their fun. Long story short, as they were leaving, they heard a woman's voice again calling out to them, and Mike was the lucky person to hear it speaking right in his ear. He claims this person was right up against his ear. He could feel an energetic presence, as if someone was truly there. The boys were so freaked that they both ran straight out of the attraction, insisting on going home. Their parents tried to calm them down, but they refused to return.

Another individual experienced quite odd occurrences on the very property where Castle Dracula used to be. Paul Bonnette was a staff member at the Wendy's that was built after the castle burned down. Today, Wendy's is no longer there, but a restaurant is sitting there on that property that is named the Shrimp Basket. As people in the paranormal field like to say, things come to life at night. Paul's paranormal experiences were true to this statement. Things started out small at first and gradually started happening more and more, such as lights flickering on and off when Paul was alone. Drink machines would start flowing and even spewing liquid randomly. Chairs and other objects, such as silverware, would be placed in various spots or put in places that would be hard to locate. It was like a game of hide and seek. Paul was told that Castle Dracula was believed to be haunted; it wasn't until he had these experiences that he started to believe that statement himself.

MARTIN HOUSE
EXACT ADDRESS UNKNOWN
PANAMA CITY, FLORIDA 32401

What comes to mind when you think of the top three most haunted locations in Bay County, Florida? Is it the Old County Jail in downtown Panama City? Is it the Holiday Inn on Panama City Beach? Is it the Martin House in

Millville? Could this county have more hauntings to offer than just three? Absolutely. Some may already be familiar with the county's hauntings from author Beverly Nield's *Haunted Panama City*. Nield covered a lot of locations that are truly haunted. Some locals are remarkably familiar with this location and its hauntings. I'd like to share their experiences, as well as the history that goes along with what is the county's top haunted location.

Millville local and true believer in the paranormal Alley Walker stated in a comments section on Backpackverse.com that she has witnessed some creepy activity while stopping by the Martin House from time to time. She claims she does believe the horrible story of what happened to the souls who once lived on this property. She claims to have seen a man, a woman and a little girl. The wife and child are seen standing by a tree in the front yard. Alley says they do make themselves known to certain people. One thing that she found to be odd is that after Hurricane Michael hit, all the surrounding trees in the yard fell perfectly around the house. Not one tree hit the house. As true believers typically feel, she was drawn to this house, as it has always been so captivating.

According to paranormal enthusiast Jonathan Ramer, many locals claim to have seen the figure of Mr. Martin standing in the upstairs window, keeping watch on the property. Some years back, someone put what looks like a gas station beer promotional cutout of NASCAR driver Richard Petty by one of the upstairs windows. This was intended as a joke, but it freaked out many young people who were looking to explore the house at the time. Imagine being startled by a cardboard cutout of a person.

Tasha Maine's family friend, a former Springfield police officer, had one heck of an experience in the Martin House. Late one night, this police officer was dispatched to the Martin House regarding a vandalism call; the alarm had also been set off. On arrival, this officer saw a woman wearing a white nightgown standing in the left upstairs window. He was aware of all the rumors about this place and brushed off the idea that this could have been someone other than an intruder. Seeing this woman as he arrived, he abruptly contacted the groundskeeper to assist with the gate so he could do a check of the grounds. As the officer slowly started walking toward the house, the groundskeeper stayed behind at the gate, refusing to go any farther. Springfield backup had arrived at the scene and stayed by the gatekeeper to assist the primary officer on scene. The secondary officer began communication over the radio to let the primary officer know that he had arrived and was there to assist if needed. Nothing was being transmitted to and from the radio. One odd thing that the keeper told the

Martin House in Springfield, Florida. *Courtesy of the Bay County Library.*

backup officer was that when you enter the building, the alarm usually goes off, and it didn't.

Meanwhile, the primary officer who initially went to investigate the scene had made it through the front doors, and they remained open. Not being able to make radio contact, the secondary officer walked toward the house and began yelling for the primary. At about that time, the front door slammed shut right in his face. He could not open the door. He began banging on the door, but nothing was happening. The next minute, he saw the primary officer running from behind the house, screaming, "She isn't real! She's the devil! Get out of here! Burn this place down!" The primary got into his car and locked all his doors, refusing to get back out. The secondary officer, still standing at the front door, turned back to the door, only to find it opening, with that same woman standing there with a baby in her arms. As he started to back up slowly, she threw the baby at him. Turning to run away as fast as he could, he heard her deafening wail. The officer made it back to the vehicles and told the groundskeeper what had happened. The groundskeeper stated, "I believe that it's all in your head." The primary officer, looking as pale as a ghost, rolled his window down to say, "I went all through the home. I made it upstairs, only to have the door shut on me and a force so strong that would not let me loose. All the lights had gone out, and there was glowing writing on the walls that appeared. On the walls were glowing, upside-down crosses and the number 666, which is known as the mark of the beast. I finally made it out, and when I went out the back door, she slammed the door and broke the windows." Both officers claim that they've never responded to a call at this location ever again.

Another individual who wanted to briefly stop by and simply experience what all the hype was about ended up having quite the vision. Devin Bush never felt he was a psychic by any means. One night, while driving through Bay County, he decided to stop by and see if anything would happen—and boy, did it. It was around 2017 when Devin pulled up in his old '91 Ford Bronco on the gravel side road that ran parallel to the Martin House. As he got closer to the first old oak tree, he began getting an excruciating headache out of nowhere. It became so severe that he had to pull over and close his eyes for a moment. As his eyes remained closed, he saw a Black gentleman who looked like someone from the early 1900s in overalls. He was hanging from a noose, dangling lifelessly from the oak tree. The emotion that came along with this vision was regret, but he also had a feeling of not being heard. Devin wondered if this was the property owner's servant. He wasn't familiar with the depths of knowledge about this location, but this experience piqued his interest in finding out more. A day later, he learned from locals about the rumor that goes along with the story of this place. A servant was caught having relations with the lady of the house, and the husband took matters into his own hands, killing the servant, his own family and then himself. While this story of what happened here is discussed in many forms, there is always truth within a haunted location—if you are willing to dig deep and do the research.

Some locals claim to have seen a lady in a white dress with black eyes lurking around the upstairs of the house. Her wailing cries can be heard not only reverberating loudly off the rooms upstairs but also echoing from as far away as the shoreline of the bayou. Many believe this house was used for séances, and some believe there is nothing here at all. According to my research, the Martin House does remain empty up on the hill overlooking the bayou.

This home was built in 1910. It once did not remain so lonesome. This house used to be filled with a family and was full of love. The stories claiming that this house is evil, filled with malevolent spirits, are considered hogwash by some. The actual house that was truly considered haunted was the original that belonged to the mother of the Martins, who lived across the bayou. Yes, the Martin family was in fact a real family, and they did stay in the home by the swamp. There was always something strange going on in the mother's home, like floating balls of lights around the property and even inside the residence. There was even a bloodstain that kept reappearing no matter how much bleach was used in attempts to remove it. The bloodstain always found its way back, seeping through the wooden stairs. There was not much of an explanation for this, other than the fact that someone had been murdered there. Eventually, this home was demolished to make the Parker paper mill.

One member of the Martin family was Andrew Martin. Andrew was the captain of a ship named *Cleopatra*, and his shipmate was a man named Bragg Butler. While making a journey in the Gulf from Port Saint Joe to Pensacola, they encountered a bad storm just outside of Mexico Beach. This storm caused the vessel to roll over, and the men abandoned it. They hopped aboard their dinghy to escape the high winds and treacherous waters. Unfortunately, the dinghy capsized, and both men drowned. Their bodies were found along the beach, covered in sand, only about 130 yards away from each other. Martin was laid to rest in the Parker family cemetery, which is not far from the home.

The remainder of the Martin family, at the time, enjoyed staying at their home on the bayou. The part of the bayou that they enjoyed the most was near the shoreline, where a dolphin visited them each day. This was a huge highlight of each day. Although the mill created opportunities within the county, it also created a great deal of pollution in the air and waters nearby. The pollution got so bad that, one day, as the family made their daily rounds of checking in with their familiar friend, the dolphin was nowhere in sight. They eventually found the dolphin washed up on the bayou shoreline, deceased. This is, truthfully, what caused the family to leave the area. They figured that if the pollution in the area was that bad, who knows how bad it could get later? The house was sold to the mill in 1951 and remains in its possession. As for the rumors about this home and the unusual paranormal phenomena here, I'll let you determine how you feel about this location. Are you a true believer that this home on the

Grave of Andrew Lee Martin in Parker, Florida. *Courtesy of Benjamin Wilburn.*

hill overlooking the bayou is haunted, or do you believe people have hyped others into thinking it is? Either way, this gorgeous plantation-style home will remain in place, waiting for its next guests to walk by wondering what it has to offer.

SAINT ANDREWS STATE PARK JETTIES
4607 STATE PARK LANE
PANAMA CITY BEACH, FLORIDA 32408

Exploring Bay County's white, sandy shoreline and gleaming Gulf waters is a huge part of what Saint Andrews State Park Jetties have to offer. Kayaking, camping, hiking, swimming, shell-gathering and sightseeing are common within this state park. Most who visit here are aware of the beauty that surrounds them, but few know of the area's historical timeline. Starting out many centuries ago, this location was used as a place for Native Americans to come and catch shellfish.

Around 1930, Shell Island was made from the Gulf Bay Pass. To locals, Shell Island is an island that is surrounded on one side by the Saint Andrews Bay and on the other side by the Gulf of Mexico. The island is a hot spot for many locals to come and enjoy some rays, take a nice dip in the water or enjoy a nice walk on the beach. Most come by boat or Jet Ski. Many anchor down for the day, enjoy the warm waters and leave just as the sun is setting. This island has sand dunes with long grass that can be seen from a distance. When I was a child, Shell Island was one of my top places to visit, no matter the season. While we sometimes visited during the daytime, there were times where we stayed overnight. My favorite memory is helping my mother anchor our sailboat, the *Leap of Faith*, just before sunset. I will never forget watching those sunsets from our sailboat with my sister, Savannah, and my mother, Janna. Nothing comes close to the sound of the horn my mother would blow just at sunset, all while the crashing waves hit the sides of the boat as we watched the sky fill with hints of orange, purple and blue. The island is a popular location for sea turtles to lay their eggs during the summertime.

World War II was significant for what is known as the Jetties today. There was a harbor defense installation that held two 155 mm guns that were implanted within the dunes in 1942. Today, one of those can be seen on the Gulf side of the jetties. According to the *Pensacola Journal*, on July 23, 1937,

Crane accident at the Jetties in Panama City Beach, Florida, 1937. *Courtesy of Bay County Library.*

there was an incident on the Jetties: one person died and three individuals were hurt during a crane accident. Arthur Smith and a crew of men were working placing the rocks that can be seen today lining the state park by the pass. Arthur was the man inside the crane when it failed to hold the weight of the rocks being placed. The whole crane came off the track, tumbling over into the water. Arthur was struck by the rocks and killed on impact. His lifeless body was pinned down by the pile of rocks until his body could be recovered. Three other people were injured when they were thrown, and some ended up with broken bones.

Most visiting this location won't know about this crane incident unless they've done their research or know a local who would tell them. Some locals and visitors claim to have heard screams while underwater coming from the rocks that line the beach at Saint Andrews State Park. Some have seen people in 1930s clothing standing on top of the rocks, trying to grab the attention of visitors nearby. As there is so much history surrounding this area of the park, I believe anyone willing to visit this location may enjoy a nice, relaxing day—or might just have one spooky experience.

CHAPTER 13

WALTON COUNTY

CAMP HELEN STATE PARK
23937 PANAMA CITY BEACH PARKWAY
INLET BEACH, FLORIDA 32413

Running from the east of Okaloosa County all the way to the surrounding counties of Bay, Calhoun, Jackson and Holmes is Walton County. This county was created in 1824 and named after Colonel George Walton Jr. An interesting fact is that one individual who signed the Declaration of Independence was George Jr.'s father, George Walton. The Euchee were the Native Americans who mainly lived within this county. Steam trains and steamboats were used to transport lumber and goods all throughout the county. Most locals believe that if the lumber, turpentine and timber industries had not been created, many jobs would not have been available throughout the county for locals. These types of jobs have created a better way of life for many individuals.

Down in the southernmost region of Walton County is a place called Inlet Beach. Inlet Beach is rumored to be the center point of a truly haunted location named Camp Helen State Park. There are many stories related to Camp Helen State Park's history, some of which are related to the hauntings that frequently happen here. On the property, there are twelve cottages and a lodge. This location has been a popular site for weddings throughout the years.

Most who visit are unaware of the hauntings that take place here. There are around three spirits that reside near the property or on it. A popular legend in the area is about the ghost of Captain Phillips of Phillips Inlet, which is often seen on and near the property. Captain Phillips's ship quickly became shipwrecked during a terrible storm. Later, he and his crew were stranded and then attacked by Native Americans. He can sometimes be seen walking the nearby trails and has even appeared in the camp's log cabin, proclaiming that this is his home. Another spirit that roams here is that of a little girl named Rose. Rose can be seen walking the beaches. She was an enslaved prisoner on Captain Phillips's ship and was eventually murdered in 1843. The spirit of a boy named George has been seen quite frequently on the property and near the pier by the house. The boy, unfortunately, didn't know how to swim and drowned in Lake Powell by the boat ramp next to the property. That took place in the early 1900s.

One individual has chosen to remain anonymous about her experience at Camp Helen State Park. The lady and her now-husband were visiting from Mobile, Alabama, for their wedding ceremony and reception. They thought this place was so incredibly beautiful that they just had to celebrate here with their family and friends. The couple had visited here previously, but they had never experienced anything like this before. The couple had decided to have their wedding in the fall, on October 28, 2015. On their arrival at the park, everything was calm and very welcoming. The groom and his groomsmen, family and friends had decided to rent out a condo the night before the wedding in the 30A area of Seaside. The bride and her bridesmaids would stay in the lodge. Part of their duties were getting the preparations ready for the wedding the next day in the lodge. After they finished setting up the lodge for the wedding the next day, everyone ran through a practice of the wedding. After the rehearsal was over, the men left and went to their bachelor party, and the women decided to hold their bachelorette party at the lodge, since they were already staying there. The ladies were downstairs in the lodge, drinks in hand, dancing around to their favorite tunes on the bachelorette playlist. They were all having the time of their lives until their music came to a halt. They each were trying to stop spinning around the room to figure out who had stopped the music on the Bluetooth speaker. Puzzled by what had just happened, they began asking each other which one of them did it and tried to turn on the music again. The music would not start. Out of frustration, one chick said aloud, "Quit messing with the music!" Suddenly, there was a man standing in the corner of the room staring at the woman with anger filling his eyes. He abruptly said, "Get out of my

The original lodge at Camp Helen State Park in Panama City Beach, Florida. *Courtesy of Florida Memory.*

home now!" Terrified by what they had witnessed, the bride called 911 to report that someone had broken into the park who wasn't supposed to be there. As the other women tried to call their significant others, each of their phones and the power in the lodge turned off. Completely in the dark and scared for their lives, the ladies screamed out for help. Then a flashlight lit up the room, and a park ranger was standing there, asking them why they were in the dark screaming. The ranger simply flipped on the light switch and reassured them that everything was fine and they were safe. Shaken up, the ladies slept with their families in the condos along 30A in Seaside. The next morning, the wedding and the reception went perfectly. Everything was fun, and the fall weather was beautiful. It wasn't until later, when the couple received the photographs from the wedding photographer of their special day, that the bride was stunned. There in the photos was that same man from the night before sitting alongside her family with the most menacing scowl on his face, complete with furrowed brows and pursed lips. This is one spooky event the couple will never, ever forget.

Many individuals and families visit Camp Helen State Park to enjoy the beauty in this part of Walton County. This area has plenty to do, whether it be kayaking, fishing, swimming or visiting these twelve cottages and the log cabin. Many people who visit tend to want to ghost hunt because of the lore associated with the land. Are you interested in looking into more of the haunted history here? Feel free to visit Camp Helen, as its gates are open year-round. Just make sure you don't open the gate to hell while you're at it!

HOTEL DEFUNIAK
400 EAST NELSON AVENUE
DEFUNIAK SPRINGS, FLORIDA 32433

About two minutes north of Interstate 10 off East Nelson Avenue is a distinctive hotel that was used as a masonic lodge for a long time. Hotel Defuniak was built back in 1920. This lodge, at one point in its history, was a drugstore and then a furniture company. Later, the lodge was remodeled as a bed-and-breakfast to create more comfort for the guests who might stop by. While the guests' comfort is important, I believe the ones who live here full time worry more about their own comfort and entertainment. This hotel is rumored to be haunted. Most guests and employees feel room 8 to be the most active. There are two children who reside within this building. One regular sound that can be heard is children singing nursery rhymes throughout the wee hours of the morning. Most hotel guests who bring their children along have their kids' toys placed in different areas, and they randomly turn on and cannot be switched back off. Others have made claims that they found their kids' toys soaking wet and no longer functioning. Locals rumor that this hotel is where two children were brutally drowned in the bath by their mother.

One individual, Scott Clark, had a different experience while staying one night at the hotel. He was about to fall asleep, and he heard a thud in the darkness. Scott didn't think too much about it until he awoke the next morning. There, in the middle of the floor, was his cell phone, perfectly placed. Scott says his phone had a rubber casing around it that gripped any slick surface and didn't slide. When he went to bed the night before, he

Hotel Defuniak. *Courtesy of photographer Jacob Whitfield.*

placed his phone on the television, which was close to the charging outlet. He later attempted to perform an experiment to see what force it would take to make his phone fall like it did. Scott says he knows for sure he didn't leave his phone near the edge. After his experience that night, his only conclusion is that his phone somehow moved on its own. He isn't sure if this could be considered a ghostly experience, but he can't explain it—he can only wonder what could have happened.

Guest Tonya Williams Welch stayed the evening with her husband at Hotel Defuniak. Tonya and her husband were lucky in getting their room, considering it was the last one available. Not knowing any of the hotel's history, they booked a room, as they needed a place to stay for the night. Late at night, they arrived and immediately said, "Wow, this place has got to be haunted." The owner confirmed that it was haunted by the tragic loss of two children who were drowned in the bath by their mother. Another person died by suicide after jumping out of the window in room 8. Ironically, this was the Welches' room for the night. That night, after falling asleep, they were suddenly woken up by the sounds of children giggling and what sounded like jacks being thrown at the door. They also experienced something jumping up and down on the bed by their feet. They most definitely had a restless night. Although they never saw the girls' apparitions, they did feel their cold presences near them. Hotel Defuniak is one of the top ten most haunted bed-and-breakfasts in Florida. Would you be able to sleep comfortably in room 8 knowing its bone-chilling past?

CHAPTER **14**

OKALOOSA COUNTY

GULFARIUM MARINE ADVENTURE PARK
1010 MIRACLE STRIP PARKWAY SOUTHEAST
FORT WALTON BEACH, FLORIDA 32548

As we approach another popular tourist destination area within the Florida Panhandle, I bet you couldn't have imagined that a marine park could be haunted. Whether it is a location near the Gulf Coast's glistening emerald-green and sky-blue waters or a location near some of the busiest of interstates, the county of Okaloosa has a lot to offer the Sunshine State. On September 7, 1915, the county of Okaloosa was created from two counties in the east, Walton and Santa Rosa. It was the fifty-second county in Florida. Some may not be aware of the meaning of the county's name. *Okaloosa* is a Choctaw word meaning "black water." Did you know that Okaloosa County's name originated from a steamboat that was used to transport people on the Black River? State representative William Mapoles introduced the first bill to help create the county. He wanted to bring more opportunities here with the fishing and lumber industries. Okaloosa County is known for its military base, Eglin Air Force Base. This base was established in 1935 and was then known as the Valparaiso Bombing and Gunnery Base.

Along the Gulf Coast, in the southernmost part of Okaloosa County, is the wonderful city of Fort Walton Beach, Florida. Named after Colonel George Walton, Fort Walton came to be during the Seminole Wars. Not only

Gulfarium Marine Adventure Park in Fort Walton Beach, Florida. *Courtesy of Florida Memory.*

is this city full of good family fun, but it is also inhabited by hauntings that could very well draw any person with a love and passion for the paranormal to this location.

Most people would see Gulfarium Marine Adventure Park as a warm and welcoming place to have some good ol' family fun. While some individuals might not be aware, there are many more things that lurk around this seaside attraction. Opening its doors for the first time in August 1955, Gulfarium became a huge hit for locals and tourists passing through. This attraction stars numerous sea creatures and even reptiles. Most of these animals were rescued, while some may have been transferred to the facility. I do believe that this facility was the first in the world to develop a synthetic milk formula. This milk formula was used to help successfully raise Gulfarium's first baby bottlenose dolphin, who was stranded at the time. What a remarkable path to create. I believe that Gulfarium still uses this method today with other rescues. A marine researcher by the name J.B. "Brandy" Siebenaler came up with an idea for this outstanding attraction. He built the main part of Gulfarium as the main stage for the dolphin show. This habitat is literally in the center of the facility. The center pool was made with parts of a steel battleship from Mississippi. It has been going strong for over sixty-five years.

Most, as they walk into this attraction, will come through the enchanting gift shop to either buy their tickets, schedule a program or even buy a souvenir to remember their fulfilling experience around this place. According to one former staff member, Allison Vanblaricum, this place is far from quiet after closing time. Allison claims there have been three deaths and one accident. A little girl was in an accident at this park. Apparently, two security guards were playing a version of Russian roulette in the snack bar around three o'clock in the morning, and most of you can figure out what happened next.

The third person to die here was a maintenance man who was working in the pump house to fix something electrical, and he suddenly electrocuted himself. While most are unaware of these deaths, some believe that these could be a contributing factor to the mysterious activities that take place here. Allison claims to have had many experiences within this location herself. She claims to have experienced activity within the gift shop as well as other areas of the park. The gift shop is known for stuffed animals being thrown when no one is present, and things can randomly drop off the shelf right in front of your eyes. Keychains and other souvenir items could be all over the floor on opening the store in the morning. Another odd thing that happens in the gift shop is that the doors are opened and closed regularly by guests who are no longer present. The doors slamming open and closed is a common occurrence. One room has an unhinged spirit who does not like anyone bothering their space. Allison personally felt this spirit one morning while opening the door to this room. This spirit traveled right through her body. Initially, she saw a distorted face and quickly became dizzy and fell ill with sickness.

Apparently, a paranormal team came into this attraction one night and stirred up quite a bit of trouble in the park. Along with what most of the staff usually encounters, the team captured an EVP of a child's laughter coming from the employee bathroom and lounge. Children's voices are normally heard around the employee showers. Most of this activity happens in the early morning hours, around two or three o'clock. When the team went to go search for whoever could have been laughing, no one was found. The feeling of being watched is one of the most common things to be mentioned when visiting here. Who would have thought that one of northwestern Florida's most popular marine life attractions could contain more than just sea life and reptiles?

JAMESON INN/QUALITY INN
151 CRACKER BARREL DRIVE
CRESTVIEW, FLORIDA 32536

If you travel twenty-six miles north of the Gulf of Mexico and head toward Interstate 10, you will approach one of the county's most popular haunted locations. If you look closely enough after passing exit 56 while driving on Interstate 10, you may catch a glimpse of this building. Originally called the

Jameson Inn, it is now known as the Quality Inn and is located in Crestview, Florida. According to an article on FrightFind.com, this location is known for its activity in room 208. This room, specifically, has caused multiple people to not only scream for dear life but also struggle to quickly jump out of bed and try fiercely to escape the decapitated woman. This woman can be seen roaming her room wearing a bleached nightgown between the hours of two and four o'clock in the morning. Some articles say that people have been woken up by hands being placed around their neck, only to open their eyes and see a headless body profusely squirting blood out of her neck. Some guests who have been brave enough to stay here have reported their luggage or other items levitating in the room and then being suddenly dropped. This room can have a disturbing smell like rotting flesh, causing guests to want to change rooms.

According to the same article, a general manager by the name of Teresa Davis can confirm that there is activity within this hotel. There is a ghost who is called Fred by the staff. Fred likes to wander on the second level of the hotel and can be seen near or even on the elevator. Some staff jokingly say, "Here comes Fred," as the elevator doors randomly open from time to

Quality Inn in Crestview, Florida. *Author photo.*

time. Suncoast Paranormal, @ShawnJD on TikTok, has several types of equipment that he likes to use while he explores the activity throughout this haunted inn. @ShawnJD has experienced cold spots, changes in energy and even some K2 hits.

Current staff member Rachelle Schmaelzle also claimed in an interview that this hotel keeps some of its staff on their toes, afraid of turning corners for fear of what may pop out at them. Rachelle stated that she felt a hand on her shoulder on the ground floor and was quite alarmed when she turned around to find no one standing behind her. A maid was doing her usual duties, cleaning up and changing sheets in a room, when she turned to see a lady standing in the corner of the room, staring her down. The maid flew down the stairs bawling her eyes out and has yet to return. One of the main occurrences that takes place is that the doors like to creak open slowly by themselves, while at other times, those same doors can be seen popping open right in front of staff and guests. Rachelle believes that there is more going on here than meets the eye but claims it is up to others to figure out if it is worth the stay or not. Would you be willing to stay at one of the top ten most haunted hotels located in Florida?

CHAPTER 15
SANTA ROSA COUNTY

COON HILL CEMETERY
COON HILL CEMETERY ROAD
JAY, FLORIDA 32565

Most visitors, when they think of the Panhandle, will mention these three cities: Tallahassee, Panama City Beach and Pensacola. While each of these cities are deeply rooted in rich history, Santa Rosa County, Florida, has substantial history as well. The Second Seminole War took place in 1838 in this county. This Seminole War was the longest battle of trying to rid the Native Americans of their land. In 1842, the county of Santa Rosa was created. The county was named after Rosa de Viterbo, a Roman Catholic saint. Although this county is full of tourism, there is still so much that is to be discovered here. In Santa Rosa County is one of the oldest cemeteries around: Coon Hill Cemetery. This cemetery originated around 1820, making it over two hundred years old. A four-foot-tall concrete wall made of gravel and stone surrounds the tombstones. It is said by many locals that this location is the most haunted in the county. This is believed to be because the cemetery is the final resting spot for many of the county's original founders. There is a multitude of remarkable individuals buried here: fifteen Civil War veterans, three postmasters, two senators, two circuit-riding preachers, two tax assessors and so many more. In fact, one of Florida's first state senators is buried here.

Coon Hill Cemetery. *Courtesy of photographer Jacob Whitfield.*

According to Tripping on Legends, there is a local legend surrounding this location. It says that anyone who visits is welcome to play an intriguing game of Humpty Dumpty with the ghosts of Coon Hill. Anyone wishing to play has a set of rules that they are meant to follow. The rules are as follows: begin at the metal gate by getting on top of the concrete wall. From there, you must walk across the wall that outlines the graves until you get to the other side. Anyone who makes it to the other side can state their victory aloud for all to hear.

The part that isn't mentioned often is that when playing, a series of challenges can occur. One of the first things people will notice when on the wall is that there is a bunch of chatter going on in the background. Often, a woman can be heard, luring you to look toward the direction of emptiness by nearby headstones. Children can be heard humming, singing or even chanting the Humpty Dumpty song. Once you make it past the first turn, you just might feel something or someone tugging on your ankles. Some have described this sense of tugging as if someone might be trying to pull you off the wall to come down with them. As you continue, you might experience being shoved off the wall, as our dear Humpty Dumpty once fell. When playing this game, at one point or another, most experience seeing a mist or fog surrounding and flowing into the cemetery. If you can successfully make it all the way around without any falls, you've won! The only problem that lies ahead of you now is the week full of horrific dreams of falling. Another interesting rumor about this legend is that women that visit this location on a full moon can become pregnant.

According to @creepycappys on TikTok, it was a hot and humid day when she visited the Coon Hill Cemetery with her sister. Without thinking about it, her sister sat on the wall, trying to catch her breath. Apparently, when sitting on the wall, her sister turned completely white and became extremely nauseous. As soon as she got off the wall, all the color came rushing back to her face as normal. Later, the TikToker, not thinking, also sat on the wall. On the spirit box, they both audibly heard, in rage, "Off the wall!" As she jumped off the wall, her stomach was in a whirl.

As stated in an article on LoveToKnow, Pensacola Paranormal investigated the secluded cemetery in April 2005. What the team discovered while on their investigation was that this location does have quite a bit of activity. On their K2 EMF meter, there were readings that reached a maximum level of five lights for ten seconds. There were cold spots all over the grounds. Sounds of shuffling and wandering footsteps could be heard all along the grass. Among all those findings, there were also the sounds of unexplainable activity.

To this day, many locals claim that this is one of those locations where taking precautions is strongly encouraged: come here at your own risk. If you want a nighttime paranormal investigation, I recommend getting in contact with the property owners and asking their permission to visit. Please don't run the risk of trespassing and getting arrested.

Some say that the hauntings at this location come to life when you least expect it. If you feel a simple game of Humpty Dumpty in this cemetery at night would give you a thrill, try this on a full moon, when all the excitement can happen! Women, beware!

IMOGENE THEATER
6866 CAROLINE STREET
MILTON, FLORIDA 32570

If you are driving on Highway 90, you will run into the city of Milton. Milton is next to the Blackwater River, which at one point in history was full of water traffic transporting goods and lumber and, in some cases, getting locals from one place to another before there were trains. Milton was incorporated in 1844 under the Florida Territorial Acts of 1844, making it one of the oldest cities in Florida.

During the Civil War era, a location just north of Milton was called Naval Air Station Whiting Field. It was mainly used by the U.S. Navy as a training field for its aviators. At one point, Whiting Field was a place where German soldiers were held as prisoners. This was also the location of the navy's first jet training unit and home to the Blue Angels Flight Demonstration Team.

Along Highway 90, near Blackwater River, where the highway turns into Caroline Street, is a location that has been one of the county's more popular buildings for many years. Built in 1913, this alluring building has overcome several troubling times of destruction. Not even hurricanes, changes in the economic growth of the city and county or even the vigorous flames that once engulfed the Imogene Theater could stop this place from success. After the 1909 fire occurred, the Santa Rosa Historical Society took over the theater and helped renovate it in hopes of keeping this location protected and locked in, as it is a part of local history. Many celebrities, such as Hank Williams, once played in this thriving Imogene Theater. Lee Ann Womack, Steve Earle and Sammy Kershaw have all been booked here. To think of these individuals being inside these walls, performing—what a feeling. It was originally named Milton Opera House; in 1921, it was renamed the Imogene Theater after the new owner's daughter. The theater has kept its name since.

This theater holds much energy, and with energy can sometimes come paranormal activity. One paranormal investigator, Tammy Misner, shared with the *Pensacola News Journal* that this place has a legend associated with it. The legend goes that a little girl can be seen throughout the building. Sometimes, she can even be seen performing onstage, like she once did for her family.

The teller of this next story wishes to remain anonymous. One night, a closing manager had quite the experience at the Imogene Theater. There were no guests or workers present in the building. There was nothing but noises that echoed in the background of the theater. As the manager walked around on the center part of the stage, he looked outward, into the audience. There, he saw the silhouette of a child standing in the back of the seating aisle. As he was trying to figure out who was in the building, he heard two sets of footsteps rush past him and stop at the edge of the stage, almost as if whatever was there had jumped off into thin air. The creepiest part is that when the manager walked toward the edge of the stage, he heard a whisper

Imogene Theater. *Courtesy of photographer Jacob Whitfield.*

in his right ear saying, "Gotcha!" Totally freaked out by this incident, the manager quickly locked up and ran for his car. He did return to work the next day but refused to stay too late after the guests left.

Some claim that this place has gentle spirits, while others are unsure if they just want to scare individuals. This location can be visited, and if you would like more historical information, a tour or information regarding this place, such as visiting hours, please reach out to either the Santa Rosa Historical Society or the property owner. If you wish to get scared, reach out to see if the owner of the building would allow your team to investigate at nightfall.

CHAPTER 16

ESCAMBIA COUNTY

PENSACOLA LIGHTHOUSE AND MARITIME MUSEUM
2081 RADFORD BOULEVARD
PENSACOLA, FLORIDA 32508

In the farthest western region of northwest Florida is Escambia County. It is also the oldest county in Florida. The county seat is Pensacola. Pensacola is often referred to as the City of Five Flags, because over the years, it has flown the French, Confederate, British, Spanish and American flags. Some locals claim that the city of Pensacola is a miniature version of New Orleans, due to all its haunting, historical and fun attractions. As many individuals travel throughout the city of Pensacola and Pensacola Beach, they may come across what is the center of this town, Naval Air Station Pensacola. This location is the home of the Blue Angels and the one and only Pensacola Lighthouse and Maritime Museum. Many service members are stationed here to learn about piloting aircraft; others are here to learn through schooling about their future jobs in the military. Many of my friends and even my own family members have been or are currently stationed on this base. I thank you each for your service and the sacrifices each of you make to protect our country.

The base is open to the public to see the practice shows of the Blue Angels, as well as explore the National Naval Aviation Museum, the Pensacola Lighthouse and Maritime Museum and Fort Barrancas. While most of these locations are indeed haunted, the place that is considered the

Top: The first lighthouse in Pensacola. *Courtesy of the Pensacola Lighthouse and Maritime Museum.*

Bottom: Aerial view of the current Pensacola Lighthouse. *Courtesy of the Pensacola Lighthouse and Maritime Museum.*

most haunted is the lighthouse. On January 1, 1859, the lighthouse was first lit. Many lighthouse towers have had to be rebuilt; the same thing happened to this one. The tower that is standing today is the second tower to have been built. This tower has 177 steps and is roughly 190 feet tall. A duplex was added to the lighthouse in 1869, and then in the mid-1890s, a passageway was connected to the tower. The views are stellar from the tip-top of this very much alive lighthouse. Some say if you visit within the right practice times, you just might get an up-close view of the Blue Angels when they come roaring through.

There are many ghost stories about this place, and one of the most talked about is the tale of the inerasable bloodstains in the southeast bedroom. It seemed that no matter what was done to change their appearance or attempt to get rid of them, they would continue to show up. The bloodstains are rumored to be from a lighthouse keeper's wife stabbing her husband to death. Some have said the remnants of blood could also be from a woman named Ella Clifford, who suffered in a difficult childbirth.

Jason Balbuena is a former lead tour guide for the lighthouse who also ran ghost hunts there. He worked for the lighthouse for four years and says he very much enjoyed it. He is also the founder of Pensacola Paranormal Research Group. Jason's experience one night took place after the board members showed up. Jason and his team had to do a rundown for them to show examples of how the tour went on. They were in the room referred to as the Bloody Bedroom, where the spirits of two children reside. One of the children, Lizzie, was around the age of nine when she passed away. During this night, Jason and his team called out to her, trying to get her to respond. Many of them heard a child's giggling surrounding them in the room. One of the board members felt someone tug on their slacks. It wasn't too much longer after this that everyone heard footsteps running in the hallway. Many of the board members were in total shock about what they experienced that night. The evidence that was recorded was enough to validate to all of us just how haunted this location truly is. Many know that there is also evidence from paranormal teams, such as TAPS and Ghost Hunters on YouTube, regarding their experiences here.

The current team lead for ghost tours in the lighthouse is Samantha Vereecke. She has had numerous experiences in this location, such as hearing footsteps in the tower after everyone left. She heard her name being called out in the breezeway. She says it's not uncommon to hear whistling, singing, humming and walking around upstairs. The basement light has a habit of coming back on once turned off and after one has walked away from the stairs. One incident took place one night in the children's room, in which someone moved a baby doll. This caused a spirit to become very hostile, unhooking the window shutters, which are usually nailed down, and slamming them repeatedly against the windows. This occurred on a night when Samantha was introducing new ghost tour volunteers—how fun.

Samantha experienced another incident on the grounds outside of the lighthouse with her coworker. These two ladies were the only people on the property and were waiting for everyone to show up for the ghost tour in about an hour. The two were sitting in the car with both windows down and the engine off. They suddenly heard a sharp whistle come from outside the driver's side door, next to Samantha's coworker. They both decided to take a stroll on a trail that leads to a giant live oak. They moved closer to the tree to see what would happen. Samantha's coworker stepped away for a moment, and when she came back, she said, "I—no joke—had hands on my throat." About that time, they both heard something moving in the woods, so they both bolted back to the vehicle. When they made it back, the other volunteers were showing up. Samantha claims this was one of the more unexplainable and intense situations to have happened on the grounds.

A visiting guest, Carl Pence, was brave enough one night to go on a ghost tour at the Pensacola Lighthouse. He was in the basement, and he used not only his spirit box to communicate with spirits but also a K2 meter. While he was standing in the basement, near the door, something suddenly started banging on the door multiple times. A few people almost tripped over their feet trying to jump back. After that incident, many individuals in the room got their hair pulled, were touched on their arm and felt they were being watched.

If you feel you are brave enough to show this location how unafraid you are, I dare you to take a nighttime ghost tour here—and feel free to check out the basement, where all the fun comes to life. Make sure to tell them that author Katlyn Jones sent you!

OLD SACRED HEART HOSPITAL
1010 NORTH TWELFTH AVENUE
PENSACOLA, FLORIDA 32501

As you drive near the downtown area of Pensacola, you just might see one of the most haunted locations in Escambia County. This gigantic Gothic Revival building is located off Twelfth Avenue and is one of the oldest standing hospitals in the Florida Panhandle. While the old Sacred Heart Hospital building is no longer used as a hospital today, a variety of businesses, restaurants and a school do operate out of it. This hospital was built in 1915 by nuns and was the first hospital to have bacterial, surgical, radiological and therapeutic facilities in the state of Florida. Before this building was erected, most people had to travel to either Mobile, Alabama, or New Orleans, Louisiana, for any sort of medical treatment. Due to Sacred Heart being overcrowded and the start of deterioration, a new hospital was built to replace this one on a different property. The old Sacred Heart Hospital was added to the National Register of Historic Places in 1982.

O'Zone Pizza Pub opened its doors in 1998 in what is allegedly the old morgue of the hospital. While some would consider this a bit morbid, most paranormal and spooky fanatics call this a spooktacular experience, as they cannot wait to get their slice of divine pizza. This place is haunted, and the women's restroom is rumored to be quite active: chatter has been heard and water faucets have turned on and then turned off, all while no one is present in the bathroom. According to a current waiter at O'Zone Pizza Pub, Paul Sackman, he had an enthralling experience one night while working his shift. He was standing at the hostess station ensuring everything was in line for the night. He had placed his notepad on the desk for a moment, and suddenly, out of nowhere, it was thrown off the countertop into the glass windowpane just by the stairs at the front of

the restaurant. Paul claims that he had no idea what could have caused this experience, but it sure had the employees on their toes.

One common occurrence at this former hospital is people seeing shadow figures near and even on the elevator. Some claim to have had their shoulders tapped on by the spirits of the nuns that roam the halls, looking for their patients. According to TikToker Allie (@spookyalliecake),

Opposite: Old Sacred Heart Hospital in Pensacola, Florida. *Author photo.*

Left: O'Zone Pizza Pub on the bottom floor of the old Sacred Heart Hospital in Pensacola, Florida. *Author photo.*

she also saw something quite unexpected. She has visited this location for many years. She was visiting one night with her friends in celebration of her nineteenth birthday. As they were looking at the artifacts on display, they turned back toward the stairs, and a man dressed in surgical attire stepped right out in front of them, stopping them right in their tracks. This gentleman was so enraged that he kept his firm gaze on them. Back when this event took place, she wasn't sure if this was truly someone playing a trick on them or if they had encountered a ghost. Now, looking back, she truly believes that this wasn't a real person, since the building was no longer a medical facility.

One of the popular things to do here is take a seat at the bar in O'Zone's Pizza Pub and enjoy a beer while chowing down one of the pub's one-of-a-kind pizzas. Don't forget, before you leave, to explore the first three floors of this very active location. There are lots of interesting trinkets and historical objects encased behind glass, just waiting to be looked at. Beware, though: do not veer past the third-floor chains with the "no trespassing" signs, or you will be arrested and charged—or who knows, maybe a phantom nun or a medical staff member just might stop you in your tracks.

CONCLUSION

Wow, I am in complete awe of the history and haunts throughout the Florida Panhandle. The northwestern region of the Sunshine State has proven to be full of paranormal stories just waiting to be heard. When I first began my writing journey, I never truly knew what to expect, as this is the first book that I've ever written. I was nervous and curious about how the book would unfold. Little did I know that through my efforts in reaching out on social media platforms and simply meeting people in my day-to-day life, I would end up with some rad ghost stories from some amazing individuals. I mean, honestly, who doesn't like hearing a good ghost story? I thoroughly enjoyed hearing about the creepy and terrifying experiences that people shared with me. These are the type of stories that should be shared around the campfire. Some stories can be considered legends and not real, but these stories are from people I've taken the time to interview and ensure that their stories are, in fact, being portrayed correctly. These are real encounters from actual people who wanted to share their stories with the world.

While writing, I did have my fair share of challenges as well. I faced harsh critics from the Bible Belt on social media trying to tear me down while I was trying to hear from people. Realizing that many people would feel this way in this region, I desperately tried to not give up or lose hope. Luckily, I had a great support system through it all.

With this book, I made it a mission of mine to truly learn and understand the history of the Panhandle. I felt that as someone who grew up here and continues to live here, I needed to know more. I have learned so much from my research about the history of this region. It's intriguing to know how parts of Florida came to be and how history has a direct effect on today's world and to think about if things had been different, there could be a totally different world around us. I was also shocked at the history I dug up in my home county. I never knew how much history surrounded the county, including how part of my family line directly impacted a small part of history here. It is my hope that by writing this book, I can encourage people of all ages to get out there in the world and investigate what your county and state history is all about. Who knows how many haunting stories could come from so many undiscovered places near you? I hope this book will bring light to many people all over the world and help people gain a better understanding of what this part of the Sunshine State has to offer.

As I truly love learning about history and the paranormal, I feel my journey must not end here with this book. Stay tuned in as I wander into the path of my next adventure.

Author Katlyn Jones off to her next adventure. *Courtesy of Forgotten Coast Photography by Layla Marie.*

BIBLIOGRAPHY

INTERVIEWS

Brown, Tanner. Personal interview, July 25, 2023.

Bryd, Greg. Personal interview, September 12, 2023.

Bush, Devin. Personal interview, July 5, 2023.

C., Jeana. Personal interview, August 26, 2023.

Hill, Mckenzie. Personal interview, June 1, 2023.

Johnson, Christopher. Personal interview, June 13, 2023.

Lane, Penny. Personal interview, July 23, 2023.

Marks, Whitney, and Oliver Marks. Personal interviews, June 14, 2023.

Martinez, Maria. Personal interview, September 3, 2023.

McCoy, Sarah. Personal interview, October 5, 2023.

Moore, Waylon. Personal interview, September 27, 2023.

Murph, Randall. Personal interview, September 19, 2023.

Pence, Carl. Personal interview, May 29, 2023.

Perry, Rebecca. Personal interview, October 22, 2023.

Sackman, Paul. Personal interview, July 5, 2023.

Schmaelzle, Rachelle. Personal interview, July 5, 2023.

Stanley, Jennifer. Personal interview, August 10, 2023.

Todd, Susan, Emerald Coast Paranormal Concepts. Personal interview, May 22, 2023.

Todd, Tracy, Emerald Coast Paranormal Concepts. Personal interview, June 9, 2023.

Vercccke, Samantha. Personal interview, July 22, 2023.

White, Frances. Personal interview, October 13, 2023.

Wilburn, Benjamin. Personal interview, July 29, 2023.

Wilson, Tyler. Personal interview, October 11, 2023.

Young, Brandon. Personal interview, August 15, 2023.

BOOKS

Cox, Dale. *The Ghost of Bellamy Bridge: 10 Ghosts & Monsters from Jackson County, Florida.* Marianna, FL: Old Kitchen Books, 2012.

Mayo, Wanda. *Ghosts of the Pensacola Lighthouse.* Pensacola, FL: Pensacola Lighthouse Association, 2008.

Nield, Beverly. *Haunted Panama City.* Charleston, SC: Arcadia Publishing, 2018.

VIDEOS

Bay County Historical Society. "Saint Andrew Bay Skirmish of 1863." Facebook, April 5, 2019. https://www.facebook.com/

Brown, Stacy, Jr. "Is It Haunted? The Warrior on the River Part 1." Facebook, October 6, 2019. https://www.facebook.com.

chazofthedead. "Have You Ever Been on a Hybrid Investigation?" TikTok, November 16, 2022. https://www.tiktok.com/@chazofthedead/video/7166717628646509870.

creepycappys. "The Legendary Coon Hill Cemetery." TikTok, May 20, 2023. https://www.tiktok.com/@creepycappys/video/7231321537968753962.

Hauntings With David. "Overnight Paranormal Investigation Inside Haunted Lodge | Wakulla Springs." YouTube, August 22, 2022. https://youtu.be/gOt6OiduAWE.

Hiking the Haunt. "Haunted Location: The Washington County News Building—Chipley, Florida." YouTube, June 1, 2020, youtu.be/G7JA7C4z2GE.

Old Panama City Beach. "A Photographic Retrospective of Castle Dracula." Facebook, April 11, 2018. https://www.facebook.com.

shawnJD. "Haunted Hotel Crestview FL." TikTok, February 14, 2022. https://www.tiktok.com/@shawnjd/video/7064701635045428526.

spookyalliecake. "Ghost or Weird Dude?" TikTok, January 23, 2023. https://www.tiktok.com/@spookyalliecake/video/7193826281643986218.

Two Egg TV. "Civil War in Apalachicola, Florida." YouTube, March 3, 2020. https://youtu.be/vlEMKwWqyzU.

———. "Ghost in the Old Calhoun County Jail." YouTube, October 30, 2020. https://youtu.be/fY7oBCqScV0.

———. "Ghost Tour of Chipley, Florida." YouTube, September 9, 2016. https://youtu.be/vdegNEVCEmY.

———. "Haunting at Prospect Bluff, Florida?" YouTube, October 31, 2017. https://youtu.be/-I1W.C.cmaCSE.

———. "Newspaper Haunting in Chipley, Florida." YouTube, October 31, 2022. https://youtu.be/JSXepfcEHMc.

WJHG Newsroom. "Time Travel Tuesday: 'Castle Dracula.'" July 26, 2022. https://www.wjhg.com/2022/07/26/time-travel-tuesday-castle-dracula/?outputType=amp.

WMBB News13. "Camp Helen State Park Said to Be Home to Ghosts." YouTube, October 31, 2019. https://youtu.be/yK8qJXndN-s.

WEBSITES

Abramo, Brandon. "The Martin House—Is It True or False?" *The Martin House Investigation* (blog). June 5, 2015. http://outsider-martin-house-investigation.blogspot.com.

Alexander, Kathy. "Fort Gadsden, Florida." Legends of America. Updated November 2022. https://www.legendsofamerica.com/fort-gadsden-florida.

Apalachicola Main Street. "Apalachicola History." https://www.downtownapalachicola.com/resources/apalachicola-history.

ARROW Project. "History: Liberty County." Florida Natural Areas Inventory. 2005. https://www.fnai.org.

Backpackerverse.com. "Haunted Bonifay: Is There an Angelic Spirit at the Waits Mansion?" September 12, 2016. https://backpackerverse.com/haunted-bonifay-is-there-an-angelic-spirit-at-the-waits-mansion.

————. "Malevolent Haunting at the Martin House in Panama City." July 17, 2016. https://backpackerverse.com/malevolent-haunting-at-martin-house-in-panama-city.

Blanks, Annie. "Paranormal Investigators Hunt for Ghosts at Milton's Imogene Theatre." *Pensacola News Journal*, October 29, 2018. https://www.pnj.com.

Britannica. "Fort Walton Beach." Last updated, February 14, 2024. https://www.britannica.com/place/Fort-Walton-Beach.

Brown, Marina. "Warrior on the River Reaches for a Helping Hand." *Tallahassee Democrat*, August 2, 2019. https://www.tallahassee.com.

Carter, Jake. "The Haunting of Palmer House." Anomalien.com. November 1, 2018. https://anomalien.com.

Castro, Gina. "The Imogene Theatre Is Booking Big Names." Ballinger Publishing. May 2, 2018. https://www.ballingerpublishing.com.

Chipley Bugle. "Homecoming at Histroric [*sic*] Hard Labor Creek Church." April 4, 2022. https://chipleybugle.com.

City of Milton, Florida. "History." https://www.miltonfl.org/244/History.

Costin, Leonard, ed. "A Brief History of the Port of Port Saint Joe." Port Saint Joe. http://www.portofportstjoe.com/port-history.cfm.

Cox, Dale. "Battle of the Upper Chipola—Jackson County, Florida." ExploreSouthernHistory.com, December 20, 2013, https://exploresouthernhistory.com/chipolabattle.html.

————. "The Civil War in Panama City, Florida." March 23, 2014. https://www.exploresouthernhistory.com/panamacity.html.

————. "Torreya State Park's Antebellum Southern Mansion." ExploreSouthernHistory.com. https://www.exploresouthernhistory.com/torreyagregory.html.

Dean, Laura. "World's Smallest Police Station." Carabelle History Museum. https://www.carrabellehistorymuseum.org/worlds-smallest-police-station.

Dehart, Jason. "This Ginormous Reptile Was Famous in Death since 1966." *Tallahassee Magazine*, May 10, 2016. https://www.tallahasseemagazine.com.

Dekle, Merritt. "The History of the Russ House, Jackson County, Florida: Introduction." July 2000. https://sites.rootsweb.com/~fljackso/RussHouse/RussIntro.html.

————. "The History of the Russ House, Jackson County, Florida: Once Upon a Time." July 2000. https://sites.rootsweb.com/~fljackso/RussHouse/HistoryRussHouse.html.

Emett, Mike. "Pensacola Hospital." Clio, September 15, 2016. https://theclio.com/entry/26205.

Enfinger, Alvin H. "Coon Hill Cemetery: Celebration of the Historic Site Restoration, October 28, 2007." Jay Historical Society & Museum. http://www.jayhistoricalsociety.org/pioneerstories/Coon_Hill_Cemetery.pdf.

Ferguson, Joseph L. "Escambia County, Florida." eReference Desk. https://www.ereferencedesk.com/resources/counties/florida/escambia.html.

Fillmon, Tim. "Saint Andrews Bay Skirmish." Historical Marker Database, last revised February 11, 2019. https://www.hmdb.org/m.asp?m=129811.

Florida Department of Agriculture and Consumer Services. "Tate's Hell State Forest." https://www.fdacs.gov.

Florida Historical Society. "Okaloosa County." April 1, 2015. https://myfloridahistory.org/date-in-history/june-13-1915/okaloosa-county.

Florida's Forgotten Coast. "Explore Apalachicola History." https://www.floridasforgottencoast.com/apalachicola-history.

Florida State Parks. "Saint Andrews State Park: History." https://www.floridastateparks.org.

Florida Travel Blog. "13 Most Haunted Places in Florida." May 5, 2023. https://floridatravel.blog/most-haunted-places-in-florida.

FrightFind. "Jameson Inn/Quality Inn." https://frightfind.com/jameson-inn-quality-inn.

Genealogy Trails History Group. "Washington County, Florida Genealogy and History." https://genealogytrails.com/fla/washington.

GhostQuest.net. "Folklore & Haunted Locations Guide: Florida, USA." https://www.ghostquest.net/haunted-places-florida-usa.html.

Haunted House Ghost. "Hotel DeFuniak Springs Florida." Facebook, January 12, 2017. https://www.facebook.com.

Haunted Places. "Jameson Inn/Quality Inn." June 25, 2014. https://www.hauntedplaces.org/item/jameson-inn-quality-inn.

Haunted Rooms America. "The 10 Most Haunted Hotels in Florida." January 29, 2020. https://www.hauntedrooms.com/florida/haunted-places/haunted-hotels.

Heard, BN. "Standing in the Road with Stephen G. Pierce." Cranks My Tractor, December 22, 2012. https://www.cranksmytractor.com/2012/12/battle-of-vernon-florida-stephen-g-pierce.html.

Hill, Beverly. "Exploring Historical Torreya State Park on the Apalachicola River Bluffs." Northwest Florida Outdoor Adventure, July 25, 2012. https://www.northwestfloridaoutdooradventure.com.

Historic Hotels of America. "Wakulla Springs Lodge History." https://www.historichotels.org.

Hotel Defuniak. "Hotel Defuniak." https://hoteldefuniak.net.

Howard. "Gregory House at Torreya State Park." *Cane Pancake Gravy* (blog). March 26, 2013. https://canepancakegravy.blogspot.com.

Hurst, Robert. "Investigating the Mystery of Old Town Spring in Panama City." *Panama City News Herald*, August 13, 2020. https://www.newsherald.com.

Johnson, Vel. "A Brief History of Tallahassee and Leon County." Tallahassee—Leon County Bicentennial. July 1, 2023. https://tallahasseeleoncounty200.com/history-of-tallahassee-fl.

Lapham, Dave. "Knott House Museum." America's Haunted Road Trip. December 15, 2014. http://americashauntedroadtrip.com/knott-house-museum.

Lehman, Candace. "What Was the Cherokee Trail of Tears?" Study.com, October 8, 2021, https://study.com.

LighthouseFriends. "Saint Marks Lighthouse." https://www.lighthousefriends.com/light.asp?ID=594.

Lindeman, Scott. "Experience Tallahassee's Spooky Side." Visit Tallahassee, October 29, 2010. https://visittallahassee.com/spooky-tallahassee.

Local Pulse Pensacola. "Step Back in Time with These Vintage Photos of Pensacola's First Hospital." April 7, 2016. https://localpulse.com.

Lodge at Wakulla Springs. "Our History." https://thelodgeatwakullasprings.com.

Lucia. "Haunted Road Trip: The Historic Sacred Heart Hospital, O'Zone Pizza Pub, & the Ghosts of Pensacola, Florida." The Ghost in My Machine, March 23, 2020. https://theghostinmymachine.com.

M., Evie. "Is Monticello Really the 'Most Haunted Town in Florida'?" NewsBreak, November 9, 2022. https://original.newsbreak.com.

———. "The Legend of the 'Wakulla Volcano' Is Absolutely Fascinating." NewsBreak, April 4, 2023. https://original.newsbreak.com.

Mackenzie, Hannah. "Paranormal History: Haunted Places in Pensacola." WEAR News, October 27, 2017. https://weartv.com.

Maddox, Kaye, and Sandi King. "The History of Bay County Florida." Beacon Learning Center. http://www.beaconlearningcenter.com.

Military Installations. "Naval Air Station Whiting Field." https://installations.militaryonesource.mil.

Museum of Florida History. "About the Knott House." https://www.museumoffloridahistory.com.

National Park Service. "What Happened on the Trail of Tears?" May 26, 2020. https://www.nps.gov/t.

Okaloosa County. "Okaloosa County Home Page." 2015. https://myokaloosa.com.

Panama City Living. "The Civil War Salt Makers of Saint Andrews Bay: The Salt of the Earth." January 15, 2014. https://panamacityliving.com.

Panama City Toyota. "Get Spooked in Panama City." December 21, 2023. https://www.panamacitytoyota.com.

Panhandle Players. "Our History." https://www.panhandleplayers.org/about-us.

Pensacola. "About Our City." https://www.cityofpensacola.com/1200/About-Our-City.

Plummer, Mike. "Saint Marks Bomber Rediscovered." WFSU Local Routes. November 11, 2021. https://wfsu.org/l.

Powell, Lewis O., IV. "A Calhoun County Haunt, Finally!" *Southern Spirit Guide* (blog), December 7, 2017. https://www.southernspiritguide.org.

Prine Pauls, Elizabeth. "Trail of Tears." Britannica, December 27, 2017. www.britannica.com/event/Trail-of-Tears.

S., Leo. "The Creepy Legend of Tate's Hell Swamp and the Curse of the Native American Medicine Man." RANDOM Times, May 11, 2022. https://random-times.com.

Sanchez, Kellie. "Meet the Ghosts of Camp Helen State Park." WJHG, October 30, 2019. https://www.wjhg.com.

Santa Rosa Historical Society. "Imogene Theatre History." https://santarosahistoricalsociety.com.

Seaman, Rob. "Saint Andrews Bay Salt Works Raids 1863." *Civil War Navy Sesquicentennial* (blog), December 7, 2013. http://civilwarnavy150.blogspot.com.

Sellers, Gene. "About the *Bugle.*" *Chipley Bugle*, December 15, 2000, https://chipleybugle.com/about-the-bugle.

These Haunted Hills. "Small Waterfall—Torreya State Park." Facebook, January 11, 2021. https://www.facebook.com.

Tripping on Legends. "The Humpty Dumpty Haunting of Coon Hill." May 9, 2021. https://trippingonlegends.com.

Unexplored Florida. "The Historic Waits Mansion." https://unexploredflorida.com.

Vanderlinden, Colleen. "The Pensacola Paranormal Society & Its Search for the Supernatural." LoveToKnow, June 7, 2021. https://paranormal.lovetoknow.com/Pensacola_Paranormal.

Visit Jackson County Fla. "Bellamy Bridge Heritage Trail." https://visitjacksoncountyfla.com/play/culture-heritage/bellamy-bridge-heritage-trail.

Visit Panama City Beach. "The Haunted History of Camp Helen State Park in Panama City Beach." October 29, 2021. https://www.visitpanamacitybeach.com.

Walton County Florida. "History." https://www.co.walton.fl.us/314/History.

Waymarking.com. "Saint Andrew Bay Saltworks—Panama City, Florida, USA." March 14, 2014. https://www.waymarking.com.

Wikipedia. "Battle of Marianna." https://en.m.wikipedia.org.

———. "Bay County." https://en.m.wikipedia.org.

———. "Blackwater River State Park." https://en.m.wikipedia.org/wiki/Blackwater_River_State_Park.

———. "Choctawhatchee National Forest." https://en.m.wikipedia.org/wiki/Choctawhatchee_National_Forest.

———. "Edward Ball (Businessman)." https://en.m.wikipedia.org/wiki/Edward_Ball_(businessman).

———. "Eglin Air Force Base." https://en.m.wikipedia.org/wiki/Eglin_Air_Force_Base.

———. "Franklin County." https://en.wikipedia.org/wiki/Franklin_County.

———. "History of Leon County, Florida." https://en.m.wikipedia.org/wiki/History_of_Leon_County.

———. "Joseph W. Russ Jr. House." https://en.m.wikipedia.org.

———. "Saint Marks Light." https://en.m.wikipedia.org/wiki/Saint_Marks_Light.

Womack, Marlene. "Shipwreck, Haunted House Linger in Memories of Martin Bayou." *News-Herald* (Panama City, FL), April 24, 1983.

WTXL ABC 27 Tallahassee News. "Looking Inside Monticello's Haunted Attractions." October 31, 2018. https://www.wtxl.com.

Yelp. "Washington County News." https://www.yelp.com.

About the Author

Courtesy of Forgotten Coast Photography by Layla Marie.

Although Katlyn Jones was born in San Diego, California, she has made Panama City, Florida, her home for over twenty-five years. Katlyn is a reiki master who focuses on healing and working at alleviating people's physical, mental, emotional and spiritual pain. After starting her paranormal team, Mysteries of the Unseen, in 2017, Katlyn immersed herself in the history and haunts of Florida's Panhandle. Through her work on her paranormal team, she started a spooky ASMR channel on YouTube called Light in the Darkness. If you'd like to subscribe to her channel, you can find her by searching for @lightinthedarknessasmr. Katlyn continues to investigate paranormal claims across her state and desires to share her finds with the world.

FREE eBOOK OFFER

Scan the QR code below, enter your e-mail address and get our original Haunted America compilation eBook delivered straight to your inbox for free.

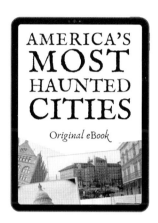

ABOUT THE BOOK

Every city, town, parish, community and school has their own paranormal history. Whether they are spirits caught in the Bardo, ancestors checking on their descendants, restless souls sending a message or simply spectral troublemakers, ghosts have been part of the human tradition from the beginning of time.

In this book, we feature a collection of stories from five of America's most haunted cities: Baltimore, Chicago, Galveston, New Orleans and Washington, D.C.

SCAN TO GET
AMERICA'S MOST HAUNTED CITIES

Having trouble scanning? Go to:
biz.arcadiapublishing.com/americas-most-haunted-cities

Visit us at
www.historypress.com